What Others Are Saying About Amanda Heal and

SEEING BY VISION, NOT BY SIGHT

"Identifying your purpose—your 'why' is something many people struggle with. During my time as a career coach, the number of times I heard someone complain about their job, yet do nothing about it, astounded me. One reason people don't change is they don't know how. They don't know how because they lack clarity. Thankfully, all of the things people lack clarity on, Amanda has written about in her book. From discovering your life's purpose right through to living that purpose and getting into action, Amanda covers it all in a well laid out, step-by-step guide. Well done, Amanda, for changing the world with your message as you continue to live your life's purpose."

— Annemarie Cross, The Podcasting Queen

"This book is packed with practical wisdom, expressed beautifully in Amanda's stories and steps forward, as she reflects on her life of building courage and discovering purpose in challenging, changing times. Take a walk with Amanda as she steps you through life's big questions with honest reflections and heartbreaking and inspiring stories—and find yourself on a purposeful, clearer path to the life you want."

— Kerrie Phipps, Speaker and Leadership Coach, Author of *Do Talk to Strangers* and *Lifting the Lid on Quiet Achievers*

"If you are searching for the purpose of your life, *Seeing by Vision, Not By Sight* is a 'must'! Clear and easy to read, yet chock-full of deep insight, this book is a wonderful tool to help affirm the meaning and purpose of your life."

— Susan Friedmann, CSP, International Bestselling Author of
Riches in Niches: How to Make It BIG in a small Market

"No one ever said creating your destiny would be easy, but Amanda Heal makes even being blind look easy. Now she shares her hard-won secrets about how to find your passion, pursue your dreams, and tackle whatever challenges try to stop you. *Seeing by Vision, Not by Sight* is a tour-de-force among personal development books. You'll revisit it again and again."

— Patrick Snow, Publishing Coach and International Best-Selling
Author of *Creating Your Own Destiny* and *Boy Entrepreneur*

"Still trying to figure out what your life's purpose is? Then check out Amanda Heal's *Seeing by Vision, Not by Sight*. The truth is we all have a purpose on this earth, but sometimes it takes a devastating event to find it. Amanda's blindness was such an event that has allowed her to see the world in ways the rest of us miss, and purpose lies at the heart of that vision—a purpose that can be yours as well when you take action on the steps Amanda suggests."

— Nicole Gabriel, Author of *Finding Your Inner Truth*
and *Stepping Into Your Becoming*

"Amanda Heal is the most able-bodied disabled person I've ever met. She has turned her total blindness into a super-power, becoming a lawyer, a life coach, a public speaker, and now an author. In *Seeing by Vision, Not by Sight*, she shares how you can also develop a vision for your future that will surpass and conquer any obstacles you face."

— Tyler R. Tichelaar, PhD and Award-Winning Author of *Narrow Lives* and *The Best Place*

"Amanda Heal's *Seeing by Vision, Not by Sight* is an inspiring, encouraging read for anyone not truly satisfied by their life or career. It's full of practical activities to help you discover the right future and the courage to embark on it. The strategies have been proven by the author's own journey overcoming obstacles that would have defeated most of us. Let her story and her practical advice stimulate you to a new and fulfilling future."

— Rupert French, Career Practitioner, Job Search Coach, and Author of *How to Get a Good Job After 50*

"This book is a powerful combination of inspiration, understanding yourself, and tangible wisdom for life. Amanda Heal manages to bridge the gap between having a vision for your life and turning it into reality, with beautiful storytelling and practical advice."

— Tash Corbin, Business Mentor

"Amanda was our guest speaker at AUSTRAC for International Day of People with Disability in November 2019. Amanda (along with her guide dog Sadie) spoke with us about the impact of digital accessibility on her daily life, as well as guide dog etiquette. Amanda is a lovely down-to-earth person, who is approachable and flexible with her talks. She adjusted her topics to suit our needs and adapted to presenting both to a room of people and via video conference stream (to our interstate colleagues) with ease. Our staff gave great feedback on her talk; we all learnt quite a lot too!"

— Breeahna Murphy Team Leader, Human
Resources Advisory at AUSTRAC

"I just had my coaching session with Amanda this evening. 'Wow!' is all I can say. I wanted/needed clarity and focus, and man, did she ever deliver! I thought I wasn't on my way towards my goals, and felt all over the place and overwhelmed. But I left the session with a solid plan, clarity, focus, and actual action steps I can do in the coming days."

— Nathalie Hotte

"I enjoyed working with Amanda Heal very much. Her enthusiasm encouraged me to set goals for myself and showed how much I could achieve in the areas of connection and communication. Amanda's coaching allowed me to set many goals, and meeting them will serve me well into the future. Thanks, Amanda."

— Daniel Pask

"Just letting you know I discovered my skills and interests through the program with you last year, after accepting a job that didn't align with those skills and interests (and hating it). I have now started working in a job that covers both my core interests and skills, and I love it! Thank you for your help."

— Eleanor Taylor-Rodgers

"Amanda worked with me in examining my career interests and direction, identifying what direction I wanted to head in, and how to utilise and embrace my unique skills and understanding to get there. She has a remarkable story and heart, and personably engages in a way that allowed me to talk through my circumstances, key issues, and ideals. We pinpointed the areas to focus on to overcome the hurdles keeping me in an unfulfilled situation. I would highly recommend engaging with her for career/life coaching."

— Jessamy Perkins

"I would recommend Amanda to help you find your purpose. When I met Amanda, I needed someone to facilitate a reconnection to my purpose, which was buried deep inside me after life-changing events. Amanda has a great toolkit, which helped propel me in the right direction; she held me accountable in a way that worked for me. Amanda helped me to see the potential ahead of me and encouraged me to stretch my goals, which then provided the clarity I needed in my career choices. Thanks, Amanda!"

— Lynda Tregoweth

"I was responsible for organising a weekly Wellbeing Phone Chat for women who have low or no vision, so I invited Amanda to speak to our group. Amanda had recently lived through a period of home quarantine after a trip overseas, and I felt her experience could help other women staying at home not to become isolated and to stay positive. As well as learning about Amanda's experience during COVID-19, the women in our group enjoyed Amanda's friendly informative presentation style, and we all appreciated her honesty in answering questions about what can be achieved in our lives, how to go about achieving our goals, and sometimes having to alter life goals when things don't turn out as we would want them to or as expected. I have no hesitation in recommending Amanda as an engaging, thought-provoking speaker, and I would like to invite Amanda to speak to a larger group of women in the future."

— Janene Sadhu, President of Blind Citizens
Australia's National Women's Branch

"Amanda first spoke to our View Club in July 2018. It was so successful she was asked to return and spoke again in October 2019. Amanda showed us that whatever difficulty you encounter in life you can overcome. I love how accomplished she is in what she achieves despite being blind from birth. She would inspire anyone."

— Junia James, President of Canberra City Evening View

"Amanda spoke to The Girls Leadership Network on finding your life's purpose and overcoming your fears. The feedback showed she helped change people's thinking in a way that had lasting impact. Amanda is an inspiring speaker. I highly recommend her for your group."

— Wendy Marman, Co-Founder, The Girls Leadership Network

"On behalf of the members of the Canberra South Branch of the National Seniors Association, I would like to thank you for coming to our meeting and giving us insight into the work of Guide Dogs, including the many different ways they assist people with vision impairment. Many of our members commented to me how much they enjoyed your talk and how informative they found it."

— Mark Redenbach, Secretary, NSA Canberra South Branch

SEEING BY
VISION

NOT BY
SIGHT

HOW TO DISCOVER YOUR LIFE'S PURPOSE AND PUT IT INTO ACTION

AMANDA HEAL

AVIVA
PUBLISHING
New York

DEDICATION

I dedicate this book to my mother, Valmai Heal, who has
stood by me like a pillar of strength throughout my life,
and who has kept me grounded and stable during the ups
and downs of the journey to discover my life's purpose
and put it into action.

I also dedicate this book to you, the reader.
I hope it brings you hope, wisdom, and peace.

ACKNOWLEDGEMENTS

This book would not have been possible without the help, support, and expertise of many people. I would not be the person I am today and would not have written this book without the teaching and wisdom of many others. Finally, this book would not be what it is without the stories I was allowed to share in it. So, I would like to thank the following people:

My lovely clients Katherine, Jennifer, and Justin (you know who you are), Subhashish Acharya, Warren Atkins, Mark Bacon, Belinda Barnier, Nasreen Bhutta, Raylee Bielenberg, Jane Boardman, Ross Bowden, Jill B. Bruce, Andrew Bryant, Glenn Butterworth, Mark and Gayle Chamberlain, Tash Corbin, Annemarie Cross, Katharina Cser, Ed Decosta, Peter Drucker, Scott M. Fay, Rupert French, Susan Friedmann, Nicole Gabriel, Roddy Galbraith, Elizabeth Gallimore, Jon Gettoes, Peter Graham, Peter Greco, Regina Green, Ray Hall, Narelle Head, my sister Lisa Heal, my father Michael Heal, my mother Valmai Heal, Ed Holicky, Nathalie Hotte, Junia James, Theresa Jennings, Anna Kazan, Janelle Keys, Robert Kiyosaki, John Klose, Dr Caroline Leaf, Christine Lockey, Sharryn Ludlow, Stacey McBride-Wilson, Wendy Marman, Paul Martinelli, John C. Maxwell, Breeahna Murphy, Kay Napier-Zanotti, Daniel Pask, Jessamy Perkins, Graham and Mandy Philipse, Kerrie Phipps, Deb Quinnell, Mark Redenbach, Janean Richards, Charles Rowland, Marjorie Roberts, Susannah Sabine, Janene Sadhu, Ella Shepherd, Christian Simpson, Stefan Slucki, Barry Smith, Patrick Snow, Eileen Tannachion, Dr Mark Tapper, Eleanor Taylor-Rodgers, Tyler Tichelaar, Ched Towns, John Towns,

Lynda Tregoweth, Shylea Ulrick, Nick Vujicic, Melissa V. West, Kelly Wood, Rick Woolcott, and my beautiful guide dogs Gypsy, Pebbles, Gillies, and Sadie.

CONTENTS

TIPS FOR READING AND APPLYING THE MATERIAL IN THIS BOOK

If you're anything like me, you firmly believe that writing in a book is a crime. However, this book is different. There are spaces throughout the book for you to write your thoughts, and I highly encourage you to use them. I recommend, though, that you write in pencil so you can make changes when necessary. Also, if part of my story inspires a particular thought, underline it so you can return to it later if necessary.

I highly recommend you read the book from beginning to end before completing the exercises. I recommend this because you will find the tools in Part II helpful in completing the process in Part I of discovering your life's purpose and putting it into action. If you can't help yourself, and just want to get started, at least skim through Part II of the book so you know what's there and where to find it when you need it.

Now, let's get started!

DISCOVERING WHAT REALLY MATTERS

"Many persons have a wrong idea of what constitutes true happiness. It is not attained through self-gratification but through fidelity to a worthy purpose."

— Helen Keller

Perhaps you picked up this book because your life feels like an endless run on a treadmill, never getting anywhere. You hate your job. You wonder whether you really have anything of worth to contribute to the world. Your future looks bleak.

Do you ever feel that your life lacks meaning or significance? Have you ever felt like you work only to pay the bills, and that your weekends are filled with chores? Do you ever wonder why you're here, or get the feeling that there's more to life than this? If you answered yes to any of these questions, this book is for you.

I firmly believe we are all put on this earth for a reason or purpose. Finding our purpose is something we are wired to do, and it's usually what makes us happiest and most fulfilled.

I've written this book because I spent a large part of my life wondering why I had been put on this earth. I was never sure what I wanted to do, so I followed the advice of family and trusted friends and took up a career in law. While, for the most part, this career choice was good, it didn't fuel my passion, and I felt there was probably more to life.

In this book, you'll discover what your life's purpose really is. You'll learn the three steps you need to take to discover your life's purpose, and how to put those steps into action. You'll find out how to find the courage you need to discover your life's purpose and put it into action, how to deal with changes that will occur in your life as a result, how to lead your own personal growth, how to master your mindset, and how to manage your finances.

I guarantee that if you do the work, follow the steps, and use the tools set out in this book, you, too, will discover your life's purpose, and learn how to put it into action. You'll realise that your life has meaning and significance, and you will feel like what you do every day matters. You'll know why you're here, and your life will be filled with excitement and possibility.

After losing my legal job, I stumbled across my life's purpose. I finally realised what I had been put on this earth to do. I've succeeded in transforming myself from an unhappy and disillusioned government lawyer to a happy and fulfilled business owner. I'm on the journey towards living the life of my dreams, and I passionately want to start you on the way to living yours!

You might be thinking you don't have the time to do the work to discover your life's purpose, or that you don't know where to start. I understand. I once thought that way too. But with this book in hand, you'll be okay. I'll guide you through each step, and it will only take a little time each day or each week to follow the process.

If you don't believe finding your life's purpose is possible, then you can borrow some of my belief. I know this is possible, and I believe in you.

So, are you ready to take the first step to discovering what you've been put on this earth to do? Are you ready to become the person you were created to be?

Don't wait another day to start heading towards discovering what you've been put on this earth to do. Don't wait another day to start living a happy and fulfilled life. Keep reading, be inspired and encouraged, and take control of your destiny by discovering your life's purpose, and planning how you will put it into action.

PART I

DISCOVERING YOUR LIFE'S PURPOSE AND PUTTING IT INTO ACTION

"Learn to get in touch with the silence within yourself, and know that everything in life has purpose. There are no mistakes, no coincidences. All events are blessings given to us to learn from."

— Elisabeth Kübler-Ross, Swiss-American Psychiatrist and Pioneer in Near-Death Studies

CHAPTER 1

DISCOVERING YOUR LIFE'S PURPOSE

"There is a plan and a purpose, a value to
every life, no matter what its location, age,
gender or disability."

— Sharron Angle, American Politician

I've always believed we are each created for a specific purpose. I
don't know where this belief stems from. Perhaps it's because I
believe in and love God, and I believe he created the universe and
all of humanity to serve his purposes.

On my twenty-seventh birthday, I was sitting at work wondering what my life's purpose was. I don't know why this happened on my twenty-seventh birthday, and not any other, but I have wondered why I am here ever since that day.

I asked my friends and colleagues for an answer, but they couldn't tell me. I asked my family, and they couldn't tell me either. I even read a book about purpose and didn't find any answers. Thankfully, I found the answer, and that is what this book is about.

WHAT IS PURPOSE?

The *Macquarie Dictionary* defines purpose as: "the object for which anything exists or is done, made, used, etc."

If you use an object for its intended purpose, the object usually works well. But if you try to use the object for a purpose for which it is not designed, it will either not work at all, or it will not work very well.

A toaster is specifically designed to toast bread and other similar products. But if you tried to make a cup of coffee using the toaster, it would not work at all. Similarly, if you used a butter knife to spread softened butter onto bread, it would work very well. But if you tried to cut steak with the butter knife, it might go some way towards cutting the meat, but it wouldn't work particularly well.

I believe the same applies to us as humans. If we discover our life's purpose, we discover the thing we are made to do, and we usually do it very well.

Pastor, author, and filmmaker Thomas Dexter "TD" Jakes describes life's purpose as being much like an instinct. It comes naturally to us—something we are wired to do. He says if we can combine our instinct with our intellect, we will obtain happiness and fulfilment.

He suggests that because we are taught to rely on our knowledge rather than our instinct, it is possible for us to live out our lives relying almost entirely on knowledge, rather than instinct or purpose. This can lead to discouragement, disillusionment, and depression.

Nutritionist and author Shawn Stevenson describes what I am referring to as a "superpower". It is a unique gift or talent that only you possess.

Presbyterian minister Stefan Slucki was born with congenital glaucoma, a condition that causes a buildup of pressure in the eye, causing loss of vision. It is relatively rare, affecting an average of 1 in 250,000 children born in Australia. If the condition is detected early, it can usually be easily corrected by releasing the excessive pressure within the eye.

Stefan had a number of eye surgeries to preserve his remaining vision, but those surgeries were unsuccessful. His parents took him overseas to have treatment, which preserved his vision for a short time, but Stefan eventually lost his vision at age eighteen.

Whilst Stefan was overseas, receiving treatment from two eye clinics in Philadelphia, Pennsylvania, in the United States, he attended a Bible college. There one of his teachers discovered that Stefan had a particular gift for explaining concepts in the Bible to others; as a result, Stefan discovered that preaching God's Word was his life's purpose.

When Stefan returned to Australia, he decided to train as a Presbyterian minister. This goal would not be easy because no blind person had ever been trained as a Presbyterian minister in Australia. However, several serving ministers had continued in ministry after having lost all or most of their vision during their parish service.

Stefan took courage from knowing a number of blind people had been trained and ordained into the ministry overseas. He had read about them in a Braille magazine, *The Braille Bible Messenger*, and was able to contact them. This was in the 1980s, before computers and mobile phones.

Stefan eventually convinced the Presbyterian Church that he should be trained, and he became the first blind person in Australia to be ordained as a Presbyterian minister. He received enthusiastic support from a Scottish-born minister who had worked alongside two blind pastors in the Highlands of Scotland and who vouched that a blind person could competently undertake this important role.

During his studies in Melbourne, Stefan became aware of another blind man training for service within the Lutheran Church of Australia, and he later met him when he began serving a parish in Adelaide.

Stefan was ordained in 1988 and is still in the ministry today. He has also served the Presbyterian Church and wider Christian community by advocating for Bible-based morally-conservative Christian ethics within government on issues such as euthanasia, abortion, marriage, stem-cell research, surrogate motherhood, etc.

When I asked Stefan how he felt now that he had put his life's purpose into action, he said:

> To live a day of life is a privilege but often involves difficulties of various kinds. I am thrilled to realise that it all has a purpose for me. All things (not just the pleasant, happy, fulfilling things but all things) work together for the good of those who love God, who are called according to his purpose (Romans 8:28). For me, that sense of every event, dark or bright, being allowed to happen to me for a reason, and a good reason at that, brings enormous comfort, calm, and confidence. God's gonna work all things out for his glory and my good. How wonderful is that!

DISCOVERING YOUR LIFE'S PURPOSE IS LIKE FINDING GOLD

I believe that discovering your life's purpose is a bit like discovering gold. Some gold is easy to find because it is on the earth's surface. It can be found in the mud of a riverbed by scooping the mud out with a pan. Once the mud is washed away, the specks of gold are left behind. Some extremely fortunate people have even picked up gold nuggets lying on the ground!

Other gold is contained within rock, hidden beneath the earth's surface. The rock must be dug out of the earth and then put through a number of crushing and refining processes to extract the gold from it.

Some people discover their life's purpose relatively easily. It is in plain sight, or just under the surface of their awareness. It isn't buried deeply, so it is easy to find, and easy to define.

Like most of us, sixteen-year-old Mark Tapper didn't know what he wanted to do when he left school. That is until he visited a chiropractor for treatment of an injury he had sustained.

Mark was so impressed with the treatment he received, and his subsequent recovery, that he decided he wanted to become a chiropractor; then he could heal people's bodies so they would function properly. He knew that was his life's purpose.

Now in his sixties, Dr Tapper is a well-known and highly respected chiropractor, and I am fortunate to be one of his patients. He loves what he does, and he is determined to keep practicing as long as he is able.

You can find out more about Dr Tapper and his services at www. belconnenchiropractic.com.

Many people must work hard and dig deep to discover their life's purpose, much like those who mine for gold underground. Their purpose is buried beneath years of a life lived doing something else. It is buried under a lifetime of old habits and beliefs. Perhaps they have dreamt of doing something, but they have forgotten their dream, or they have been told they could never pursue or achieve it. Perhaps they never knew what their life's purpose was.

Jennifer had always loved music, and she had been involved in playing some type of music since she was three years old. Whether she was performing in a school band, playing duets on the piano with her brother, or singing alone or in a choir, there was always music in her life.

Jennifer had always dreamt of being a professional musician, but she was discouraged by her peers from pursuing her dream because they thought she probably wouldn't be able to earn a stable income as a professional musician. She also wasn't sure whether she was really good enough to be a professional musician. So, Jennifer eventually forgot about her dream.

After finishing school, Jennifer started working for a telecommunications company. She worked for the same company for quite a number of years, and she mostly enjoyed the work. However, she was eventually moved to a position in the company where she quickly became very unhappy. The pressure was constant, and she felt unappreciated by her supervisors. Eventually, this situation began to take a toll on her health, so Jennifer took a severance package and left the company.

Without the pressure and unhappiness of work, Jennifer found she had more time to think deeply about her future. She then remembered her dream to be a professional musician.

After much soul-searching and working with a coach (me), Jennifer realised her life's purpose was to serve and bring joy to others through music and writing. She found the courage she needed to start on her journey towards putting her life's purpose into action.

Jennifer got a part-time job and started studying for a graduate certificate in music. She loved it so much that she continued on to complete a graduate diploma.

Today, Jennifer plans to put her life's purpose into action through writing, recording, and performing music, and also writing inspirational material.

When I asked Jennifer how it felt to be on the journey towards putting her life's purpose into action, she said, "I feel like a completely different person. I have been transformed, reenergised, and I'm so much happier. It feels like a new beginning."

THREE STEPS TO DISCOVERING YOUR LIFE'S PURPOSE

What I'm about to share with you is my distilled learnings from three years of stumbling around, searching for my life's purpose. If you follow these steps, your journey will hopefully be shorter and more focused than mine, and you'll discover your life's purpose sooner and with more clarity than I did.

I believe there are three steps you need to take to discover your life's purpose. They are:

1.   Examine your present.

2.   Examine your past.

3.   Examine your passions or dreams.

You might want to undertake a psychometric or personality test, such as Myers-Briggs Type Indicator, or DISC, to assist in this examination. These tests tell you quite a lot about your behaviour in different situations. Many such tests are available, and they serve different functions, providing different results.

Some of these tests can only be performed by psychologists while some are available online for free or for a small fee. Others are facilitated by trained professionals, such as life coaches and career counsellors.

You might be asking, "How do I examine my present, past, and passions?" You can do this several ways, so I'll tell you about the method that works for me. You can then adapt it to best suit yourself.

First, it's important to choose the right environment for this process. Sometimes, I think better lying down or sitting comfortably in a quiet place with no interruptions. Other times, my thoughts flow more easily if I'm doing something repetitive with my hands, such as simple knitting. Other people have told me they think best while they are walking.

Secondly, you must ask yourself a specific question. It would not be something broad like, "What is my purpose?" Rather, it must be narrow, perhaps a particular aspect of the broader question such as "What things did I most enjoy doing when I was a child?" or "What makes me feel the happiest and most fulfilled right now?" I like to ask God the question, but you can ask yourself, the Universe, or anyone you prefer.

Thirdly, you have to wait for the answer. Continuing to ask the question over and over again, or somehow striving for the answer, will not do you any good, much like trying desperately to remember someone's name won't bring it to your mind. Just ask your question and wait.

I wouldn't necessarily call this waiting period "meditation"—it's more of a relaxation of the mind. I don't try to think of anything, but I don't try not to think of anything either. If an irrelevant thought comes in, like "What am I going to have for dinner?", I let it pass through without dealing with it. It's like letting a rope or piece of yarn run loosely through my fingers.

Eventually, something relevant comes through. It may be an answer or a related question. I take hold of it and ponder it for a while. Sometimes, I will let it go and wait for another thought, but other times, it leads me down a path of consideration and discovery.

Sometimes, if I'm stuck on a tough question, I need to store it away for a while and come back to it later. I like to think of this process as being similar to putting a tough piece of meat into a slow cooker to stew for a while. When I return to the question hours or even days later, it is much easier to deal with, and I can often draw really good answers from it, much like how the slow cooker tenderises and draws flavour from the meat.

Finally, it's a good idea to record particularly good thoughts or decisions. You can use a pen and paper, a computer, or perhaps a recording device, such as a phone. If you're worried that recording your thoughts in detail will interrupt the flow of thoughts, just re-cord a word or two to jolt your memory later. After you've finished, you can write everything out in full. If you know you'll be able to return to your thoughts, you can pause your thought process, re-cord whatever you've decided or come up with in detail, and then restart from where you left off.

Throughout this book, I will ask you questions to help you in this examination process, and I will provide space for you to write your answers.

Be aware that following the steps above to discover and refine your life's purpose will require some deep thinking on your part, and it will take some time. But I promise that every minute you spend, and every ounce of effort you put into this process, will be worth much more than you ever expected.

Your life's purpose is a broad thing: to serve, to entertain, to work in nature. The way you put your life's purpose into action is what makes it uniquely yours.

I didn't discover my life's purpose all at once, but my life's purpose and the way to put it into action have gradually been revealed over time, and they are still being refined. However, my life's purpose is becoming clearer and more exciting to me every day, and I have no doubt yours will too.

EXERCISE

1. Now that you have read this chapter, do you have any ideas or thoughts about what your life's purpose might be? If so, write them down below. If not, that's okay. Keep reading; it's still early in the process.

    _____

    _____

    _____

    _____

    _____

    _____

2. Do you know whether you have any skills or abilities that could be characterised as your gifts or superpowers? If so, write them down below. If you can't think of any, read on; some questions in future chapters may help with this.

    _____

    _____

    _____

    _____

    _____

SUMMARY

If you discover your life's purpose, you discover the thing you are made to do. Some have described this purpose as being like an instinct, while others have described it as being like a superpower. If you can discover your life's purpose and put it into action, you will live almost by instinct, and you will enjoy the life you were created to live, obtaining maximum happiness and fulfilment.

Discovering your life's purpose is like refining gold. Some people find their life's purpose is just on the surface while others discover it is buried beneath a life of doing something else.

To discover your life's purpose, you need to examine your present and past, and your passions and dreams. This examination process involves choosing the right environment, asking specific questions, waiting for the answers, and recording them in some way, perhaps in this book. This process may take some time.

Your life's purpose is a broad thing: to serve, to entertain, or to work in nature. It is the way you put your life's purpose into action that makes it uniquely yours.

CHAPTER 2

EXAMINING YOUR PRESENT

"If you don't like the road you're walking, start paving another one."

— Dolly Parton, Country Singer and Songwriter

In Chapter 1, I discussed the meaning of purpose and how different people discover their life's purpose. I outlined the three steps I believe you need to take to discover your life's purpose, which are to examine your present, examine your past, and examine your passions and dreams. In this chapter, I will deal with the first of these steps—examining your present.

WHY DO YOU NEED TO EXAMINE YOUR PRESENT?

Examining your present is vital because it shows you where you are, much like the "You Are Here" arrow on a map. Like when navigating with a map or GPS, you need to know where you are before you can work out how to get where you want to go. Examining your present also gives you an idea of how you might like to put your life's purpose into action; it allows you to determine what is working for you now and what is not.

Examining your present can reveal a lot about you. It is an opportunity to get to know yourself extremely well, and it can give you a chance to take stock of what you have and what you might be lacking.

I've had to examine my present a number of times over the years, mainly because I didn't know what I was doing, and I didn't have the benefit of a structured process, like the one set out in this book.

The first examination of my present was thorough, but I was only looking at my present from the perspective of someone about to lose their job. I was not examining my present from the wider perspective of someone searching for their life's purpose.

You may find you need to return to examining your present while you are refining how to put your life's purpose into action, but if you do this process thoroughly the first time, your subsequent examinations will be much easier; then you will only need to look at what has changed since you examined your present the first time.

WHAT IS WORKING NOW AND WHAT IS NOT

When I first looked seriously at my present, I was about to lose a job I hadn't enjoyed for years. I knew I wanted to do something different, but I didn't know what.

I did know some things, though. The parts of my job I enjoyed most involved helping people find solutions to problems. I enjoyed writing, and my recent supervisors had told me I wrote well. Also, I enjoyed giving training and presentations to my colleagues.

I knew I had not been happy in my job for a couple of years, and I felt undervalued and unappreciated by my supervisors and clients. Most importantly, I no longer felt what I was doing was making a difference.

EXERCISE 1: WHAT IS WORKING NOW AND WHAT ISN'T?

When answering the following questions, reflect on as many areas of your life as possible, such as your career, relationships, environment, faith, and finances. Pay particular attention to what is working for you right now and what isn't. In each case, consider why that thing or area of life is or is not working, and what you would like to change. Write your answers in the spaces below.

1. When was the last time you felt happy and fulfilled? What were you doing and who was with you?

_____

_____

_____

_____

2. What do you enjoy about your current job and why? What do you dislike and why?

_____

_____

_____

_____

3. What do you enjoy in your personal life outside work and why? What do you dislike and why?

_____

_____

_____

_____

4.   Are you happiest in a crowd, in small groups, or alone? If in
      a crowd or small group, whom do you most enjoy spending
      time with?

_____

_____

_____

_____

In 2013-2014, the Australian Public Service made cuts to many
government departments and agencies. Many departments and
agencies laid off large numbers of employees. In addition, a job-
freeze meant no new jobs were being created, and no one could
apply for promotion.

During this time, people asked me if I was afraid of losing my job.
I laughed and said, "The government will always need legislative
drafters. Besides, I'm totally blind, a woman, and a union delegate.
They wouldn't dare!" How wrong I was.

In late 2013, management advised my drafting area that half of us
would lose our jobs and that all legislative drafters would have to
reapply for their jobs.

I'm usually the sort of person who deals with a crisis by talking to others about it. But I was so shocked by the announcement that all I could do was sit in my office and sip water. I didn't want to talk to anyone because I was afraid I would cry. The desire to cry increased when I heard someone else burst into tears in the corridor outside my office.

After the initial few minutes of shock passed, my mind started filling with questions: Why should I have to apply for a job I won on merit seven years ago? What happens if I can't keep my job? Should I take a package or apply for another job? What happens if I can't get another job? How on earth will I pay the mortgage without a job? My disability meant that I couldn't just go out and get some casual work in a supermarket or delivering pizzas until something better came along.

As these questions filled my mind, fear set in. I was brought up to believe that a job in the Australian Public Service was a job for life and I would always have job security. I felt as if the rug were being pulled from under my feet, and I didn't know what to do.

Soon, the workday was over, and I went home. It was then, alone in my house, that the tears came, and the fear of the unknown overwhelmed me.

I'm certainly not someone who can pluck scriptures out of the air, word perfect, complete with the correct Bible reference. I wish I was. I'm more likely to say, "I think there's a scripture somewhere in the Bible that says something like…".

So, I was surprised when, in the midst of my tears, the reference Jeremiah 29:11 popped into my head. I looked up the verse, and the first thing that surprised me was that the reference was correct! The second thing that surprised me was the words I read were relevant to my situation. For those unfamiliar with this particular scripture, it reads, "'For I know the plans I have for you,' declares the Lord, "plans to prosper you and not to harm you, plans to give you hope and a future.'"

Then something even stranger happened. An almost audible voice in my head said, "I have a job for you." I should also say that, back then, I wasn't someone who heard from God very often.

Skeptics may say this experience was wishful thinking. However, both the Bible reference and the words were completely unexpected and unsought because I was still in shock. I found they gave me instant comfort, and I was able to visit my family and let them know what had happened without any further tears.

Soon after, I went through the process of reapplying for my job. It was one of the hardest job application processes I'd ever endured. I still had a sense of entitlement to my job, so it was almost impossible for me to put my whole heart and soul into writing the application, which was the only way I had been successful in applying for jobs in the past.

The written application I submitted was not as good as it could have been, and the interview did not go well. Needless to say, I was not successful in keeping my job. I got the news five days before Christmas.

Not only was I a member of the Commonwealth Public Sector Union, but I was also a union delegate. I can't adequately express my gratitude for the support the Union gave me during my last six months as an employee of the Australian Public Service.

Shortly after Christmas, a friend contacted me to say she was holding a business launch. On the day before the launch, management announced it would offer severance packages to those who had been unsuccessful in keeping their jobs. This threw me into another bout of feeling miserable and rejected. The next day, I decided to attend the launch so I "could get some champagne and sympathy".

I got the champagne and sympathy I needed, and I was also able to support and congratulate my friend on the launch of her new business. It turned out the business was with a network marketing company that sold beautiful, natural, anti-aging skincare products for the face and body.

I was not new to network marketing; I had sold Tupperware for a year or so, a long time ago. I listened to the presentation with interest, and even tried some of the products.

I decided very early on in the launch that I wasn't going to buy any-thing because I was happy with my current skincare regime. But after I tried the products, I changed my mind. They felt beautiful on my skin and smelt great!

A thought flashed through my mind: Perhaps starting a business of this type could be an alternative to waiting until I got another job. I quickly put this thought aside, though, because my parents had always told me that remaining in government employment was the best option for me. So, if I started a network marketing business, it would be a hobby, just as selling Tupperware had been. I asked the consultant who ran my friend's launch to give me a week to decide what I would do, and I went home with a sample pack of skincare products.

The evening was warm, so, when I got home, I took my phone and a glass of wine out onto the deck to think about what had happened during the business launch. As I sat there, I experienced a flash of realisation. Perhaps staying in government employment wasn't the only opportunity for me. With a job-freeze on, there was no guar-antee I would get a job I liked, or even get a job at all. Maybe a slim chance existed that I could do something outside of government.

I googled the phrase "What do I do when I lose my job?" Imme-diately, an article came up about a woman who had lost her job, and the process she went through to decide what she wanted to do. After a year of searching, she had started a business and was doing well. Perhaps I could do that too. But what sort of business? Would it be network marketing, or something else?

I thought back to the time I had met and spent quite a bit of time with a handful of successful business people. I had admired them for their achievements and wished for that freedom and lifestyle for myself. Since meeting them, I had secretly wanted to run my own business, but I had never allowed myself to think seriously about it because I had a "good, stable job". Finally, I allowed myself to wonder whether I should leave the Australian Public Service and run a business. I felt I shouldn't limit myself to network marketing, but also look at other business alternatives.

TAKING STOCK OF WHAT YOU HAVE

It is good to take stock of what you have right now. If you do this thoroughly, you will probably be surprised at just how much you really do have. I'm not talking about physical stuff here; I'm talking about your personal attributes that make you unique, and that you can offer to the world.

I took stock by using CareerStorm Navigator, a set of web-based career and life development tools that engage people into honest and meaningful dialogues about their career and life objectives. Using the tool, I was able to look at four areas of my life—interests, skills, values, and personal qualities—and rank my answers in each area to come up with my top five. I was then able to rank different career choices against different combinations of my top five interests, skills, values, and personal qualities.

Whilst CareerStorm Navigator is a tool primarily to help people examine their career options, I believe it can also help to examine life more broadly to discover your life's purpose. Your interests, skills, values, and personal qualities are what make you unique, and they can point you to your life's purpose. So, let's look at each of these areas in turn below.

INTERESTS

Looking at your interests can help you identify your most important expertise. Your interests are also the things that make you happy when you pursue them. One of those interests will turn out to be related in some way to your life's purpose.

I wrote down a huge number and variety of interests ranging from food and travel to recording my voice and even volcanoes.

EXERCISE 2: WHAT ARE YOUR INTERESTS?

1. List your current interests in the space below. To help spark ideas, consider the types of books you like to read, the types

of TV shows and movies you like to watch, your current hobbies, etc.

_____

_____

_____

_____

2. In the space below, list any past interests you are not pursuing now. Consider past hobbies.

_____

_____

_____

_____

3. In the space below, list any interests you haven't yet explored. Consider things you would like to find out more about.

_____

_____

_____

_____

SKILLS

These skills are skills you can transfer from one part of your life, such as a career or hobby, to another. By using your skills in whatever you do, you'll be at your happiest because you will be doing what comes naturally to you. As with interests, one of your skills will be very closely related to your life's purpose.

I was amazed just how many skills I had, and how many of them were transferable. As a lawyer, I could write well, was a good empathetic listener, and could speak in public reasonably well. I could deal with people, could formulate a good argument, and had a good structured way of thinking. When I looked at the different ways I could use those skills, I could do all sorts of things career-wise.

EXERCISE 3: WHAT ARE YOUR SKILLS?

Questions 1-4 relate to your skills, and questions 5-8 relate to your superpowers (see Chapter 1). Write your answers in the spaces provided.

1. What are all the skills you use in your current job?

    _____

    _____

    _____

2.   If different, what are the skills you have used in previous jobs?

_____

_____

_____

_____

_____

3.   What creative skills do you have?

_____

_____

_____

_____

_____

4.   What skills would you like to explore in the future?

_____

_____

_____

_____

5.   What are your unique gifts or talents?

_____

_____

_____

_____

6.   What things do others tell you you're good at that you do with
      ease?

_____

_____

_____

_____

7.   What are things you do without thinking because you just
      can't help yourself? e.g., solving others' problems.

_____

_____

_____

_____

_____

8.   What are you naturally drawn to? e.g., music, numbers, words, others' problems, adventure, risk, service, or laughter?

_____

_____

_____

_____

VALUES

In early 2020, I had the pleasure of interviewing Values and Culture Expert Jackie Le Fevre on my podcast. Jackie says we each live in a world of our own construction, where our values exist in a dynamic relationship with our underpinning beliefs. Our underpinning beliefs are things about which we are highly certain, and our values are feelings that attract or repel us from certain things.

Jackie explains that our values perform like the neck of an hourglass, through which information flows into us from the outside world. We make sense of that information based on who we are in our world. Our values filter out things that have no meaning for us, and get us to focus on the most significant things. That's how they can then drive our behaviour.

It makes sense then, that if your values attract or repel you from certain things, and affect your attitudes and behaviour, they will be very closely connected with your life's purpose.

I highly recommend taking the values inventory at www.magmaeffect.com. It is a much more thorough way to discover your values than by merely picking words from a list.

EXERCISE 4: WHAT ARE YOUR VALUES?

1.   If you clearly know what your values are, list them here.

_____

_____

_____

_____

2.   How closely does your life align with your values right now? Write your thoughts below.

_____

_____

_____

_____

PERSONAL QUALITIES

Your personal qualities reflect the way you work and live your life, and your approach to work and life in general. Interestingly, the qualities you admire the most in others are qualities you possess yourself, or that you would like to develop in yourself.

EXERCISE 5: WHAT ARE YOUR PERSONAL QUALITIES?

1.   In the space below, list all the people who have had the biggest effects on your life, and the personal qualities you admire most in them.

    _____

    _____

    _____

    _____

2.   What are your personal qualities? List them below.

    _____

    _____

    _____

    _____

After completing the CareerStorm Navigator process, I frantically researched all the careers I could think of that used the skills, interests, values, and personal qualities I had discovered. Careers I considered included editing, technical writing, professional blogging on food and travel, and tutoring.

The problem with all of these, except for blogging, was that, while I certainly had transferrable skills, I didn't have previous experience or relevant qualifications. My friend's network marketing business kept coming up as the winning choice, so I signed up as a skincare consultant. In hindsight, I wish I had done this examination process with a view to discovering my life's purpose, rather than just finding another job.

As soon as I left the Australian Public Service, I threw myself into my network marketing business. Before signing up as a consultant, I asked friends and colleagues if they would hold or attend workshops for me. Many said yes, so I got off to a good start.

With most network marketing businesses, not only are product sales important, but so is recruiting new members into the business and obtaining a steady stream of workshop or party bookings to continue selling products and recruiting others into the business. I was not very good at obtaining bookings or recruiting, so once my initial clients had purchased their products, my sales quickly dried up.

One of the main ways the company taught us to get clients was to engage strangers in conversation. Gradually, we brought the conversation around to either what the person did for work, to determine whether they might need extra income or even a new job, or towards something to do with skincare or makeup. Then we gave them a product sample to try.

This method of seeking out clients and recruits challenged me on several levels. Firstly, I didn't get out much. I shopped for groceries, worked out at the gym, and went to the hairdresser, but that was about it. Also, striking up conversations with random strangers was difficult for me because I couldn't make eye contact, and I couldn't use the recommended conversation starter of complimenting the stranger on something, e.g., their shoes, hair, makeup, or clothing. Obviously, I could tell someone they smelt nice, but where do you go from there? I even tried eating out in cafes, but that did not guarantee someone coming up and talking to me, so I didn't do it much.

I also tried meeting potential clients through networking events. I didn't fully understand that the purpose of networking was not necessarily to gain clients, but to obtain referrals, so I quickly became frustrated when no business owners wanted to buy my products, and I stopped going.

As the months passed, my self-confidence fell lower and lower. I began to resent the success of colleagues who were doing well. But

I couldn't give up. I had told everyone network marketing was what I was going to do, and I didn't want people believing I was a failure. Worse still, I didn't want to return to the Australian Public Service with my tail between my legs to get a "proper job", as some of my friends suggested.

About six months after leaving the Australian Public Service, I came across another consultant, in the same business as me, Wendy Marman. She was offering personal development training to the Canberra-based consultants. Wendy taught me that to grow my business, I needed to grow myself first, particularly in the area of leadership. Her courses were based on the teachings of John C. Maxwell, a world expert in the areas of leadership and personal growth. I signed up.

The concepts in those courses changed my life! I learnt that to be a leader, I had to:

- Learn something every day.
- Lead by example.
- Act in a way that encouraged respect and trust.
- Value people for who they were rather than what they could give me.

Over the next twelve months, I gradually applied these principles to my life, and, while my business did not grow, I did.

EXAMINING MY PRESENT AGAIN

In July 2015, I fell and seriously injured my knee. I underwent emergency surgery and came home from the hospital in a splint from my hip to my ankle, which remained on for the next two months.

My recovery gave me a lot of time to think. I took a good, hard look at my present situation. Eventually, I admitted to myself that I wasn't doing at all well in my business; in fact, I was losing more money than I was making. I didn't have enough clients, and I wasn't willing or able to do what it took to get more.

As far as I could see, I had three options:

1. I could keep doing what I was doing, and be unhappy.

2. I could return to paid work in the Australian Public Service, which was out of the question because I felt I could not bear to go back to full-time work for an employer.

3. I could change businesses. But what could I do?

Then Wendy contacted me. She told me she had observed my personal growth over the past year and asked if I would be interested in joining the John Maxwell Team to retrain as a John C. Maxwell Speaker, trainer, and coach. After much discussion and prayer, I agreed. So began the most intensive training of my life.

I received broad training in five areas: leadership, speaking, coaching, mindset, and building a business around masterminds and workshops, and I was encouraged to start thinking about which of those areas I would specialise in. All my life, I had found public speaking very easy. I had even considered becoming a motivational speaker on cruise ships. This role combined two things I loved—travel and encouraging people. So, I decided to specialise in public speaking. I had enjoyed Wendy's coaching and training, and I had seen her use her coaching skills to help and encourage others. So, I specialised in coaching as well.

Once I completed training, I needed to decide what I would do with my new qualifications. As I pondered this, I had a flashback to when I had had to choose whether to take the severance package or not. I remembered how uncertain about my future and how terribly alone I had felt then. I knew I wasn't the first person, or the last, to go through this process, but at the time, I had felt that no one understood what was happening to me.

All of a sudden, the thought hit me: I wanted to help people who were miserable in their jobs or facing job loss to find out what they'd love to do, and to help them gain the courage to do it! I never wanted anyone to experience the feelings of fear, loss, and rejection I had experienced. I wanted to walk beside people as they went through that difficult time, providing guidance and support, and also opening their minds to all the possibilities out there. My second business had begun, and I think this was the first glimmer of my life's purpose.

For the next eighteen months, I did everything I knew to get clients—posting regularly on Facebook, Twitter, and LinkedIn; attending networking events; handing out business cards; running free webinars; and even recording fifteen episodes of a podcast. While I did obtain a handful of clients whom I loved working with, my business could hardly be described as thriving, and I was spending much more money than I was making.

EXAMINING MY PRESENT ONCE MORE

Towards the end of 2017, I became incredibly disillusioned and began to wonder whether I was meant to be a career coach. I spent more and more time doubting my abilities as a coach and trainer, and I thought that perhaps I wasn't getting work because I wasn't good enough.

This thought soon became a self-fulfilling prophecy. I had invested a large portion of my savings in advertising on Google, and I was regularly receiving phone calls from potential clients. But every time it came to getting them to sign a contract to work with me for three months, they pulled out.

Nearing despair, I stumbled across a coach in Florida named Regina Green. Regina was running a free webinar called "The Unstoppable You". The title grabbed my attention, so I signed up. Throughout the webinar, Regina asked questions about what participants thought of themselves, whether they doubted their abilities, and whether they were searching for success and not finding it. It was as if she were inside my head, reading my mind.

I never contributed or commented in webinars. But during this one, I couldn't type my questions into the chat box fast enough. Before the webinar had even finished, I had booked an appointment for a free "Discovery Call" with Regina. Within the week, I had signed up to work with her for three months.

With Regina's help, I discovered the reason I wasn't getting work was because my own doubts and negative self-beliefs were driving clients away. While I tried my best to be confident and positive, the words I used in my social media posts and my tone of voice on the phone were somehow conveying self-doubt to my potential clients. Worse still, I had become afraid of getting clients, in case I let them down by not being able to deliver what I had promised.

After a lot of soul-searching, I realised I was afraid I would let clients down because I didn't feel qualified as a career coach. While I was well-qualified as a general life coach, I didn't feel I had the specific career-related skills required of a career coach. I realised I wanted to focus on the person's whole life rather than just their career.

Once I discovered this, everything changed. I felt set free from the "career coach box" I had placed myself in. I suddenly became excited about what I was doing, and I lost all fear of not being good enough. But I wasn't quite there yet. There were still steps I had to take to discover my life's purpose.

SUMMARY

Examining your present is important because you need to know where you are before you can work out where you want to go. Examining your present will give you a good chance to get to know yourself really well and discover what is working for you right now and what is not.

You may find you need to return to examining your present while you are refining how to put your life's purpose into action, but if you do this process thoroughly the first time, your subsequent examinations will be much easier.

You can take stock of what you have by discovering your interests, skills, values, and personal qualities. These are what make you unique, and they are all closely related to your life's purpose.

CHAPTER 3

EXAMINING YOUR PAST

"I'm trying to get to a deep
future, but in order to get to
a deep future, I had to think
about the deep past."

— Mary Daly, American Radical Feminist,
Philosopher, and Theologian

In Chapter 2, I discuss the first step to discovering your life's purpose—examining your present. In this chapter, I will discuss the second step—examining your past.

WHY IS IT IMPORTANT TO EXAMINE YOUR PAST?

Examining your past can tell you a lot about yourself. As you reflect on as many areas of your life as possible, pay particular attention to what worked for you and what didn't. In each case, consider why that thing or area of life did or did not work for you, and why. Examining your past will give you an idea of how you might like to put your life's purpose into action.

If you look at your past from the outside, through the eyes of a keen observer, you will notice themes. These may include patterns of thought, reactions to various situations, likes, dislikes, and preferences. If you examine your past with a reflective, questioning mind, you will begin to see the "why" behind some of these themes.

The reasons behind your actions and reactions will relate to the interests, skills, values, and personal qualities you discovered in Chapter 2, and they may even bring up some new ones. If so, feel free to go back and record these in the spaces in Chapter 2.

EXAMINING MY PAST

In Chapter 2, I told you how I had begun working with a life coach, Regina Green, and how I discovered I didn't want to help people figure out what they wanted to do in their careers, but in their lives in general. This was a huge revelation to me, and I knew I would need some time to process it and work out how I would do it. What better place to do so than on a cruise aboard the *Pacific Explorer*! This holiday had been booked months earlier, of course, but the timing was perfect.

My mum and I always cruise together, and as usual, the first full day at sea was a busy one, spent exploring the ship. After lunch, though, Mum decided it was time for a nap, and as she dozed, I lay on my bed and started to wonder about what was unfolding as I worked with Regina. Was it my life's purpose to help other people discover theirs? How could I help people discover their life's purpose if I didn't know what mine was?

I didn't know the three steps for discovering my life's purpose, of course, but for some reason, I started to reflect back on my life, starting from the previous day, and going right back to my early childhood. Rather than bore you with every detail of my life in reverse chronological order, I will tell you about the themes I saw running through my life, and how I discovered them.

OVERCOMING CHALLENGES

I've never seen myself as being particularly courageous. But others have commented to me that they do. I do know, however, that I am rarely put off by a challenge.

As I mentioned earlier, I am totally blind and have been since birth. I'm the sort of person who, if you tell me I can't do something, will often find a way. I think this theme started right from my birth.

THE CHALLENGE OF SURVIVAL

I was born, as one of twins, on 6 March 1970. My mother had been hospitalised with a high-risk pregnancy sometime before, so when she started haemorrhaging early on the morning of our birth, we were able to be delivered quickly by Caesarian section.

Poor mum didn't even know she was having twins, as they didn't do ultrasounds until twenty-six weeks back then, and we were born three days before her ultrasound was due. They also did emergency Caesarians under a general anaesthetic, so she was very surprised to wake up and find out she had not the one expected baby, but two.

At birth, I weighed 1 pound 9 ounces (0.70 kilograms) and my twin sister Lisa weighed 2 pounds 3 ounces (0.99 kilograms), and we were both 10 inches (25 centimetres) long.

Mum didn't have the benefit of being given steroids before our birth, so our lungs were underdeveloped. Therefore, we had to be put into special humidicribs to keep us warm and provide us with oxygen. We were both very fortunate because the Royal North Shore Hospital, where we were born, had just received two brand-new humidicribs, the latest on the market, which would provide us the oxygen and warmth we needed to survive.

Many years later, one of my friends had premature twins. She was able to get special permission for me to go and touch them in their humidicribs. This experience was absolutely mind-blowing for me because I was able to get some sense of what Lisa and I would have looked like and the environment we would have been kept in when we were born.

Despite having the latest available technology and care, the fight for life was too much for Lisa; she died about ten hours after she was born. Sadly, back then, parents were not encouraged to hold their babies after they died, so mum never got to hold Lisa. Even sadder, she wasn't well enough to go to Lisa's funeral.

I, on the other hand, was not going to give up easily. The hospital matron had to make tiny mittens and booties for me because I kept trying to pull the tubes supplying with oxygen and milk out of my nose.

The hospital was undergoing extensive renovations at that time, so the workers could see into the nursery. My dad was upset that I was completely naked, so the nurses made nappies for me out of tissues, which they fastened with a tiny gold safety pin.

When I was three months old, my parents were finally able to bring me home. Even then, I only weighed five pounds, or 2.26 kilograms. My parents never suspected anything was wrong with my eyes until they took me to the paediatrician soon afterwards. He referred me to an ophthalmologist, who diagnosed me with having Retinopathy of Prematurity (ROP).

ROP is a potentially blinding eye disorder that primarily affects premature babies weighing about 2 pounds 12 ounces (1.25 kilograms) or less, who are born before thirty-one weeks. The smaller a baby is at birth, the more likely that baby is to develop ROP.

ROP occurs when abnormal blood vessels grow and spread throughout the retina, the tissue that lines the back of the eye. These abnormal blood vessels are fragile and can leak, scarring the retina and pulling it out of position. This situation causes a retinal detachment, resulting in vision impairment and blindness.

One risk factor for ROP is a high level of oxygen in the humidicrib. These days, oxygen is very closely monitored, and babies' eyes are tested soon after birth, so the incidence and severity of ROP is lower than when I was born. Treatments are also available today that can halt ROP's progress, especially if given early.

I am very grateful I was given too much oxygen rather than too little so I didn't suffer brain damage. I'm also very grateful and thankful to the staff at the Royal North Shore Hospital who cared for me over the three months I was there.

CHALLENGES AT SCHOOL

When my parents came to live in Canberra in late 1970, all blind children were sent interstate to attend special schools for the blind. My parents got together with some other parents of blind children who lived in Canberra and lobbied the government to integrate all the blind children in Canberra into a normal school rather than have them sent away.

This lobbying was successful, and it was decided all the blind children would be integrated into a single school so all the resources—specialist teachers, Braille transcribers, special equipment, etc.—could be pooled. This arrangement worked well, and I was the youngest among a group of four blind students to be fully integrated into Turner Primary School.

The first day of school I met Ella. We were inseparable from that day on. Ella was my best and only friend. We did everything together. She was my guide since long canes weren't given to very young children back then. Now long canes are routinely given to toddlers. So, Ella was my guide, my friend, my confidant, and my helper.

Ella and I spent so much time together that in grade 5, the teachers decided it would be better for us to be separated and put in different classes. I was using a long cane by then and could move around the school independently. Ella and I were both so upset that the following year, our parents demanded we be put back in the same class, which we were.

I felt a bit apprehensive about starting high school because I knew it was so much bigger than primary school, and the children were so much older, but I knew everything would be okay because Ella and I were going to the same school. However, the week before high school started, my entire world was turned upside down. Ella's father contacted my parents to tell them Ella was, in fact, not going to Lyneham High School; the family had decided to move to Goulburn, a country town about two hours' drive from Canberra, so she would be going to school there. It still makes me sad to remember this; I cried for days.

All the excitement and anticipation I had felt about high school evaporated and was replaced with anxiety, and even fear. It didn't help that the week before school started, I had to spend hours learning how to get from place to place in the school building, knowing Ella wouldn't be there to help me if I got lost.

One consequence of having Ella as an exclusive friend was that I never developed the skills necessary to make friends. I had also pushed away anyone who had tried to befriend me because I felt I didn't need them. Consequently, when I got to high school, I had no friends, even though most of the people in my classes had come from Turner Primary School and I knew them. Those four years of high school were the loneliest of my life, and ones I'm glad I will never have to repeat. I had no friends and few social skills, and I felt lost in a sea of hormonal teenage humanity, where I just didn't fit in.

Being the logical person I am, I decided one day, standing outside of maths class, that it would help me to make friends if I could talk with the other students about something we had in common. I listened to the conversations going on around me and determined the most popular subject was music.

So, it became my mission over the next four years to learn absolutely everything I could about every popular song and artist around at the time. I listened to the most current and up-to-date radio station we had in Canberra, and the popular Australian television music show *Countdown* became compulsory viewing on Sunday nights. I got to the point where I only had to hear a few bars of any '80s song and I could instantly tell you who wrote it and I could sing the chorus. While this strategy didn't win me any new friends, I spent a lot of time listening to and enjoying music, so it added a lot of pleasure to those years.

My lack of friends meant I mostly spent my breaks alone at school. But rather than worrying too much about it, I would read my textbooks, which certainly didn't hurt my academic progress.

Unsurprisingly, one of my favourite subjects at school was music. I also sang in the school choir, learnt piano, and played trumpet in the school band.

You may wonder how I read music. Well, there is a Braille music code. It uses the same system of dots used in literary Braille to represent the musical notes, and then uses other combinations of dots to show length, pitch of notes, and other musical symbols.

The trumpet is usually held in two hands, with the left-hand taking most of the weight of the trumpet and the right hand pressing down the valves or keys. Because I needed to read the Braille music, I held all the weight of the trumpet with my right hand, and read the Braille music with my left hand. The trumpet would become quite heavy after a while!

I also couldn't use a traditional music stand because it would be at the wrong angle and height for me to comfortably read the Braille music with my fingers. So, my wonderful friend, music transcriber, and teacher, Ross Bowden, built a special music stand for me. Imagine a tabletop the size of an A4 sheet of paper, with a metal rim around the edge. This tabletop screwed onto a single leg that screwed onto a round base. This was my music stand, and it worked beautifully for me for many years.

When I played the piano, I couldn't read the music and play the same way I could when I played my trumpet, so I had to memorise the music bar by bar. Consequently, if I hadn't played a piece for a while, I would forget it and have to relearn it.

The subject I hated most was physical education (PE). My poor PE teachers didn't really know what to do with me. I was bad at anything athletic, and I couldn't play the sports we were taught during high school.

To their credit, my PE teachers did their best. They provided me with circuit training type activities to do whilst the other students were playing sports, but these quickly became very lonely and boring. Consequently, I did everything I could to get out of PE lessons—forgetting my PE clothes or shoes, or getting a sick note from Mum—whenever I possibly could.

One part of PE I did enjoy were the dancing lessons we had one term. The dances were mainly square and circle type dances, where I was in contact with someone else most of the time, and participation was easy and fun.

I'm still slightly traumatised, though, by one incident when I stepped on my partner's shoelace, which had come undone, and fell on top of him! The music stopped, and there was complete silence for a second or two, and then everyone laughed! I always hated dancing after that.

This story does have a happy ending, however. Many years later, a friend of mine took up ballroom dancing and encouraged me to join. I eventually did, and I spent a number of very happy years becoming a reasonably accomplished ballroom dancer, progressing up to gold medal standard in Latin dancing.

While I hated the first four years of high school, the last two were an absolute joy. I changed schools, so I had the chance to start again with a completely different group of people. I made friends quickly, and I am still friends with most of them today.

CHALLENGES OF OVERSEAS STUDY

While in high school, I had the opportunity to gain work experience with a physiotherapist. I loved it and decided I wanted to pursue physiotherapy as a career. So, I tailored the last two years of high school towards studying it at university, taking on a heavy load of maths, physics, chemistry, and English.

When I contacted the physiotherapy schools in Sydney and Melbourne to investigate the possibility of studying with them as a blind student, the staff at both schools threw up their hands in horror and said they couldn't possibly take me on. This was prior to the passing of the Commonwealth *Disability Discrimination Act 1992*, so there was not much I could do.

Then, a blind friend of mine told me about a school in London, England, the North London School of Physiotherapy (NLSP), which specialised in training blind students to be physiotherapists. I applied to study there.

The British academic year didn't start until September 1988, and

I had finished school in December 1987, so I had nine months to kill. I lazed around for a while and did a small amount of voluntary work. Then I got the opportunity to work with a physiotherapist for three months as her assistant. It was great!

My mum had spoilt me as an only child, and I had never learnt to cook, clean, or care for my clothes. If I was going to live overseas, I would have to learn a few things. So, I spent six weeks at a specialist centre for the blind in Melbourne, learning daily living skills.

Part of the application process for the NLSP involved physical and written tests. The written tests I passed with ease. I didn't do so well on the physical tests, but I was given no indication of this at the time.

These were no ordinary physical tests. There were normal tests of fitness, like jumping jacks, squat thrusts, and running on the spot, but I also had to walk along a balance beam. Strangest of all, I had to put four stools in a square with a space of four feet between them, and then place a fifth stool in the centre of the square without touching any of the other four. I found this a challenge, but I tried my best. I also had to walk beside a wall, keeping a certain distance from it without touching it.

I was finally accepted into the NLSP. Mum and I travelled to London, along with mountains of Braille books, a cassette player, laptop, Perkins Brailler (a Braille typewriter), and many other things.

About eighteen weeks into the course, we were all interviewed and told whether we were allowed to continue with our studies. The first eighteen weeks turned out to be a probation period.

Only then was I told I hadn't done well in my physical tests. I had been unable to balance on the beam, and I had failed the test with the stools. Based on those tests, the teachers at the NLSP suspected I had spacial awareness problems, meaning problems determining where objects are within space. However, they never told my parents or me about their suspicions, so we had raised £16,000 to pay for my board and tuition at the NLSP.

I was told my spacial awareness problems would hinder my ability to work as a physiotherapist in the hospital system; therefore, I would not be allowed to continue my studies at the NLSP. I should return to Australia as soon as possible and "study something more academic". The crazy thing is most blind physiotherapists I have met over the years have gone directly into private practice on qualifying, so they have been able to set up their work environments to suit their needs.

I was devastated. That phone call home to my parents back in Australia was one of the hardest I've ever had to make.

My aunt, who lived in Devon, in the southwest of England, traveled to London to help me pack up everything. I returned to her house and stayed there until my mum could get a flight over to bring me and my mountains of equipment back to Australia.

Soon after arriving at my aunt's house, I remember sitting in her living room, crying, and wondering aloud what I was going to do. All I'd wanted to be for the last three years was a physiotherapist. Now that was impossible.

My aunt said, "You've got a good brain. Why don't you become a lawyer?"

I asked what lawyers did since my only experience of lawyers was sitting quietly beside my parents at the age of eight as an elderly lawyer read out my grandfather's will. I knew they did something important, but that was it. I vaguely remember my aunt talking about a friend of hers who was a lawyer, but I don't remember the details.

Thankfully, before travelling to London, I had applied and been accepted to study commerce at the Australian National University in Canberra. I had no intention of studying commerce because I wanted to be a physiotherapist, but on my dad's advice, I had applied, been accepted, and deferred my studies for a year, just in case. What good advice that was! So, I returned to Australia and enrolled in commerce at the Australian National University.

I was happy enough studying commerce because I knew something about what an accountant did, and I thought it wouldn't be a bad job to have. However, in my first tutorial, I felt a little unsettled. The tutor asked everyone why they had decided to study commerce. Everyone else said they wanted to work for "Such and Such" accounting firm, or they had always wanted to be an accountant. When it was my turn, I didn't know what to say. I mumbled something about liking numbers.

In my second year of commerce, I studied Introductory Business Law. The lecturer was a delightful man and one of the best storytellers I've ever come across. He brought cases to life. I can honestly say I can't remember a lot of the law I learnt in that course, but I certainly remember the stories behind the cases! I always looked forward to his classes and thoroughly enjoyed them. They were much more interesting than the accounting and economics courses I was studying.

Then I remembered my aunt's suggestion to become a lawyer. I went to the Dean of Law and asked if I could transfer from commerce to law. The dean told me that because I had a "credit" average (i.e., above a "pass") in commerce, I could transfer to law. However, the law faculty did not encourage people to study straight law. They preferred that students combined their law degrees with something else. The dean suggested I add law to my commerce degree and make it a combined degree, rather than transferring from one degree to the other. This combined degree would normally take five years to complete, but I chose to take a slightly lighter course load, and complete my combined degree over seven years.

I am so grateful for all of the help I received from my dad, particularly in those early years of my university study. He was retired by then. He showed me where my new lecture theatres and tutorial rooms were each year, and he took me to the library so I could borrow books for essays, which he would read sections out of onto cassette tapes. He also visited the faculty offices and got me the handouts and other materials in advance, and he spent hours photocopying chapters of textbooks so we could convert some material into Braille, and have others read onto cassette tapes by an army of amazing volunteers.

It wasn't possible to get all the material put into Braille due to the time this took, and the cost. Although I had some government funding for this process, it was still quite costly for me. So, the only things we had put into Braille were handouts and occasional diagrams from textbooks.

The rest of the material was read onto tape, with varying levels of success. Whenever one volunteer reader would reach a table with more than two columns in it, she wouldn't even attempt to read it. Others would try in vain to describe economics graphs as "sort of an L-shaped thing with two lines crossing like an X".

My favourite reader, particularly for economics, was a retired maths teacher, Mr Atkins. I loved maths, so I found it really easy to understand his description of graphs as he described them in mathematical terms.

The large chunks of text between the graphs were very dry and boring for me, as they were for Mr Atkins. He would indulge in a glass or two of red wine to help him get through the chapter. Needless to say, I could sometimes hear a subtle change in his speech by the time he reached the end of a ninety-minute tape! I must say, though, that it was only because of Mr Atkins that I passed economics at all!

I was also very fortunate to come across another volunteer, Mrs Gallimore, who read economics, law, and accounting for me for many years. There was nothing she was afraid to tackle, and I was very sad when she left Canberra to live closer to her family.

Most of the material I had translated into Braille consisted of balance sheets and profit and loss reports. Because Braille is much larger than print, only thirty-two characters can fit across one page. So, the Braille transcriber invented an ingenious way of constructing these tables, which would often stretch across two and sometimes three Braille pages. She would Braille the columns on separate pages, and then stick the pages together with sticky tape, or punch holes in the pages and tie them together with string. The whole table could then fold in on itself to make it into a more manageable size, much like a glossy brochure folds into thirds.

Consequently, to properly read these tables and understand the spacial relationship between the columns of numbers, I would often spread them out on the floor and kneel down to read them, using a ruler to line up the columns. Even with the ability to read spreadsheets using a computer with a screenreader today, I still appreciate having had the physical experience of reading those Braille tables because it made it easier to imagine the layout of spreadsheets in my head.

Fortunately, I was able to get extra time, and my own room, to do my commerce exams because I would often have to read parts of the exam paper on the floor as described above. I would sometimes have to construct my own tables in a similar way, providing notes to the Braille transcriber who would join the sheets together, and then write in print over the top of my Braille answers so they could be marked by my lecturers.

In the last few years of my law studies, the National Library, and later the Canberra Blind Society, purchased document scanners that recognised printed text and converted it into speech, which I would record onto yet more cassette tapes, or into text files I could read on my computer. My father would spend many hours scanning in books for me. But he would have to cover up the footnotes with paper because they would not scan well for some reason. I eventually bought my own scanner, and I would spend my summer holidays scanning in the books for the following year.

As technology improved, the Australian National University purchased a Braille embosser, and it would emboss all my law exams in house. However, when they embossed the first exam, something had been set incorrectly on the embosser, so the exam was embossed in another language. It was like that nightmare I'm sure every student has had at some point of sitting an exam and turning over the paper to realise it is in a foreign language. Only, for me, it was for real!

I still had extra time for my exams, and my own room, complete with an exam supervisor. So, when I mentioned to her that I couldn't read the paper, she very kindly suggested that perhaps I had it up-side-down and I should try reading it the other way round. I had already tried this, but I tried it again just to make sure. She ended up having to read me the paper so I could complete it. This never happened again, thankfully!

After five years, I graduated with my commerce degree. My first guide dog, Gypsy, was allowed to come up on stage with me and graduate too, which was great! Two years later, when I graduated with my law degree, my second guide dog, Pebbles, graduated with me. Someone even made a cap for her! I always used to say that one dog had a commerce degree, and the other had a law degree.

CHALLENGES OF WORK

By the time I finished my studies, I had the very strong impression that any lawyer worth their salt would obtain work in private practice because work in government was for those who couldn't make it in the private sector. This was a rather sad misconception because work as a government lawyer was interesting and varied. I imagined I would get a job as a commercial lawyer in a private firm when I finished university.

Back in the days when I applied for my first job, all job applications were submitted in hard copy. I enlisted the help of a company that specialised in getting employment for people with disabilities. I wrote a generic application letter and CV and asked the company to send them to every law firm in the phone book, which they did. I was determined to get a job without reliance on a government traineeship or program for people with disabilities. I felt that, with a degree in commerce and a degree in law with honours, I should be able to get a job on my own merits. I had no idea that I would need to submit 147 job applications before I received a job offer.

As it happens, I only got the position because I knew someone who knew someone who was working in the government agency offering the job. The lady's contract was about to end. She contacted me and asked if I would like to come in for an interview. And so, I began my seventeen-year career as a government lawyer.

The challenges I faced during my legal career were numerous and varied, but they mainly centred around obtaining information.

In the early days, research was difficult because most legal material was not available online. If I wanted to look something up, I had to find the relevant pages in the correct law report or loose-leaf service and scan them.

The loose-leaf services were contained in large folders of pages, portions of which could be replaced as the law was updated. Rather than being contained in ring-binder-type folders, a number of spikes ran from the bottom cover of each folder, up through the pages, and then clipped onto the top cover, which could be removed when the pages had to be replaced. This meant the folder could not open flat enough to scan the pages on a flatbed scanner.

Late on the second or third day of my first job, I was scanning some of the pages from one of the loose-leaf folders. I had detached the top cover and turned over a hundred or so pages and stacked them neatly on top of it. I was in the process of placing one of the pages onto the scanner to read when my elbow bumped the stack of pages on the cover, and the whole lot fell on the floor. Horrified, I bent to scoop up the pages when my colleague exclaimed:

"Don't touch them! Just leave them and go home, and I'll fix it".

I'm proud to say that in seventeen years of law, I never dropped a loose-leaf service folder again, and I never put the pages back out of order.

Another challenge for me in the early days of my career was faxes. They were originally printed on thermal paper, which would fade over time, to the point where I could not scan them. Also, the quality often wasn't very clear. I often had to ask clients to email or post me photocopies of the documents, or I would ask someone to read the faxes to me.

Many of my clients didn't know I was blind. Unless I had difficulty with a document I couldn't read, the subject never came up.

But one day, I was faxed a photo that had to be attached to an affidavit I was drafting. When I asked my colleague if the photo was clear enough, she laughed and said it was a blob with arms and legs and that I should call back the client and say I could see as much of the photo as my colleague, and I was blind. I did, and the poor client was so embarrassed that he refused to speak to me for two years! Thankfully, he eventually forgave me.

Another client asked me if he could send me his photo. I agreed, and he emailed it to me. I called him back later, explained that a colleague had described the photo to me because I was blind, and asked him a question about it. He apologised profusely and begged me not to sue him for discrimination. I thought the whole thing was hilarious!

CHALLENGES OF BUSINESS

I've already told you a little about the challenges I faced obtaining customers in my first business in network marketing and how I started a business as a coach.

The main challenge I've faced in business has been social media. Facebook, Instagram, and even Twitter are such visual platforms. When I talk about this in my speeches, I like to joke:

"You sighted people are so demanding. Not only do you want me to post pictures on social media, but you expect them to be the right size, and the right way round!"

I should add here that my Twitter banner was upside-down for about six months before someone told me. I'm also very careful about which photos I post to social media from my iPhone because I once accidentally shared a photo of a bank statement on Facebook.

An absolute game-changer for me in business and life in general is AIRA (Artificial Intelligence Remote Assistance). AIRA is a wonderful service that enables me to use an app to contact a specially trained AIRA agent, whose job it is to describe what my iPhone camera is seeing, or what is on my computer screen.

AIRA agents have helped me with many daily personal tasks, such as identifying clothing and medication and even finding my bird when she got out of her cage and wouldn't come back when I called her. But they have also helped me position content on web pages, correctly position myself before making a video, and choose photos for a slide presentation.

PUBLIC SPEAKING

A recurring theme I have noticed when I look back over my life is public speaking. I've never understood the paralysing fear some people experience at the thought of speaking in front of others. My parents talked and read to me constantly from the time I was born. Thus, I started talking early and, at the tender age of three, would sit proudly up at the bar in my dad's army mess and request a gin and tonic. Of course, the bar staff gave me a soft drink, but I didn't know the difference, so I thought I was very grown up, having the same drink as my dad!

When I was on the high school debating team, we did quite well. After one debate where I was second speaker for the affirmative team, the judge gave his comments on our debates. Much to my dismay, he said, "I thought the second speaker for the affirmative team gave a very good speech. It's only a shame it was delivered to the wall instead of the audience."

At university, I had the opportunity to do some PR work for Guide Dogs NSW/ACT. It involved speaking to school and community groups, and even being interviewed on TV. I was so relaxed and comfortable during an interview on a national lunchtime talk show that I crossed one leg over the other and let my shoe hang from my toes. This wouldn't have been a problem, except that the camera was focused on my guide dog, lying at my feet.

When my good friend, who got me into dancing, got married, I was honoured to be one of her bridesmaids. Just as we were about to walk into the reception, the groom realised no one had been allocated the job of proposing the toast to the groom's parents. As the groom and best man fretted over what they would do, I stepped forward and enthusiastically volunteered.

During dinner and the other speeches, I quickly formulated a plan—thank the best man for his toast to the bridesmaids, give a couple of reasons why I thought the bride and groom would have a long and successful marriage, and then propose the toast to the groom's parents. The only problem was I was afraid I would forget the parents' names. So, during the other speeches, I elbowed the second groomsman every few minutes and whispered "John and Shirley?" Thankfully, everything went well. I must have done a good job because the bride cried as she thanked me afterwards.

Soon after I finished my coaching and speaking training, I was invited to work as a paid public relations speaker for Guide Dogs NSW/ACT. I jumped at the chance because it was an opportunity to promote the organisation that had given me three guide dogs (at the time of writing, I'm on my fourth), and it was also an opportunity for me to use my newly acquired speaking skills.

As a PR speaker, I talk to all sorts of different community groups and organisations about guide dog etiquette and the services that Guide Dogs NSW/ACT provides. This is an absolute joy!

ENCOURAGING OTHERS

I think I've wanted to help people in some way since I was young.

When I was five or six, Mum asked me, "What do you want to do when you grow up?"

With the great confidence of a five-year-old, I replied, "I want to be a nurse." I think this was probably because Mum had been a nurse.

"Why do you want to be a nurse?" Mum asked.

"Well," I said, "nurses put bandages on people and make them feel better."

Not wanting to crush my spirit, Mum replied, "That's true, darling, they do. But nurses do lots of other things as well. They make lots of beds, and you don't like making beds, do you?"

"No," I said.

"And they also empty bedpans," Mum continued.

I asked what those were, and Mum explained.

"Oh, no! I don't want to do that!" I exclaimed in horror. No more was said on the subject.

During high school, I was fortunate enough to gain work experience in quite a number of fields. But the ones I enjoyed most were occupational therapy, speech therapy, and physiotherapy because they all involved practical ways of helping people. This work experience piqued my interest in becoming a physiotherapist. While I wasn't helping individuals as a government lawyer, I preferred to think of my clients as individuals I was helping, rather than representatives of government departments.

All my life, people have told me I inspire and encourage them. This used to frustrate me because I didn't understand why they said it; I was just being me and living my life. The frequency of these comments began to increase when I started speaking and coaching.

But then one day, I attended a conference and had the privilege of hearing Nick Vujicic speak. He was born with no arms and no legs, and no one knows why. As I listened to him speak, I thought how great it would be to talk to him afterwards. The first thing I'd do would be to tell him how inspiring and encouraging I found him.

I chuckled to myself as I realised I wanted to say the one thing to Nick that frustrated me when people said it to me. I suddenly understood I wanted to say this because it was how I felt, and when people said it to me, it was how they felt. I didn't have to understand why people found me inspiring or encouraging—they just did, and that was okay. I didn't get to meet Nick that day, but I am grateful for the lesson he taught me.

While I sometimes have trouble with my own doubts and negative self-talk, I have absolutely no difficulty encouraging others when they struggle with doubts or limiting beliefs. Similarly, while I'm not always quick to recognise my own achievements, I regularly find myself praising others for theirs, or thanking people for a job well done.

Once, when I was overseas with my mum, we were waiting in a hotel lobby for a coach to pick us up and take us on a tour. We had not stayed at that hotel, but it was the designated meeting point for the tour. As we arrived, Mum commented that there were no lights on in the hotel or in any of the buildings across the street. We found out someone had run into a power pole a block or so away, so all the nearby buildings had been without power for most of the night.

It broke my heart as I listened to guest after guest angrily demand their money back and check out of the hotel because they had no power or hot water. The receptionist spoke to each one with courtesy and never lost her patience. I knew I had to break the torrent of abuse with some kind and encouraging words, so as our coach pulled up, I went over to the desk and told her how sorry I was that the guests were being so rude to her and that she was doing a truly amazing job handling them all so calmly. Mum said this made the receptionist smile.

RETURNING TO THE PRESENT

Back on the *Pacific Explorer*, Mum was awake and asking me why I was perched on the edge of my bed looking so excited. I tried to explain that I had just gone on a journey back through my life and discovered some themes running through it that perhaps pointed toward my life's purpose. As I did my best to articulate everything I'd discovered, I realised I still had a lot of thinking to do.

But I'd done enough deep thinking for the day, and happy hour was fast approaching. So, it was time to get changed into something a little less casual and find a bar for a drink or two before dinner.

EXERCISE

Now it's your turn to look back over your life. Write the answers to the following questions in the spaces below. Make a note of any themes you discover because they will point to your life's purpose, and how you will most likely put it into action.

1. In what past situations did you feel most happy and fulfilled? What were you doing, and who were you with?

    _____

    _____

    _____

    _____

    _____

2. What previous careers or jobs have you enjoyed the most and why?

_____

_____

_____

_____

3. Which careers or jobs have you disliked the most and why? In each case, can you turn these dislikes into things you would have preferred? For example, you might dislike being micro-managed and prefer independence or autonomy.

_____

_____

_____

_____

4. What are some past hobbies and interests you've enjoyed the most and why?

_____

_____

_____

_____

5.   What holidays have you most enjoyed and why?

_____

_____

_____

_____

6.   Have you exercised any superpowers in your past that you've forgotten about? (See Chapter 2).

_____

_____

_____

_____

SUMMARY

It is important to examine your past because it will tell you a lot about yourself and point you towards your life's purpose.

If you look at your past from the outside, through the eyes of a keen observer, you will notice themes. If you examine your past with a reflective, questioning mind, you will begin to see the "why" behind some of these themes.

Looking back over my life, the themes I observed were my ability to overcome challenges, a love of public speaking, and the ability to inspire and encourage others.

CHAPTER 4

EXAMINING YOUR PASSIONS AND DREAMS

"I've learned over the years that when I go to that place of passion within me, there's no force in the universe that can interfere with my completing a project."

— Wayne Dyer, American Self-Help Author and Motivational Speaker

I n Chapters 2 and 3, I discussed the first two steps to discovering your life's purpose—examining your present and examining your past. In this chapter, I will discuss the final step: examining your passions and dreams.

WHY IS EXAMINING YOUR PASSIONS AND DREAMS IMPORTANT?

Just like your present and your past, your passions and dreams can tell you a lot about yourself. Your passions can give you clues about what your purpose might be, and your dreams can give you clues about how you might like to put your life's purpose into action.

Many people say to me, "I'm not passionate about anything", or "I don't have any dreams". The truth is, we all have passions and dreams. The problem is many of us have squashed them or put them aside for so long that we have forgotten about them.

The *Macquarie Dictionary* defines passion as: a strong or extravagant fondness, enthusiasm, or desire for anything.

In her Let's Reach Success blog (https://letsreachsuccess.com/2015/09/12/describe-passion/), Lidiya K suggests that passion means something different for every person, and it can't be put into words. She says it's the reason you wake up with enthusiasm in the morning, and it moves you so much that it makes you cry.

Writer, business owner, and coach of high-performing CEOs Craig Ballantyne defines passion in this way: "It's amazing what you can do when you are consumed by passion. Wake up early. Work long hours. Skip meals. Focus with laser-sharp intensity. And get up early the next day and happily do it again."

The late Sam Walton, the American businessman and entrepreneur who founded Walmart, once said: "If you love your work, you'll be out there every day trying to do it the best you possibly can, and pretty soon everybody around will catch the passion from you—like a fever."

When I talk about dreams, I'm not talking about pie-in-the-sky-type dreams, which are wild ideas with no strategy or basis in reality. I'm also not talking about idealistic dreams of how the world would be if you were in charge.

The *Macquarie Dictionary* defines a dream as: a hope that gives one inspiration; an aim.

Anatole France, winner of the Nobel Prize for Literature, once wrote: "To accomplish great things, we must not only act, but also dream; not only plan, but also believe."

Early on in my legal career, I met a couple who had successfully run several businesses and invested their income. They had reached the stage where they had enough passive income to live on, and they only worked in their businesses occasionally to keep them going.

They piqued my interest in the possibility of running my own business and enjoying that sort of lifestyle.

I had no idea what I could do (running my own law practice never occurred to me), but I knew I loved the idea of being in charge, not answering to anyone else, nor depending on anyone for my success.

As I grew older and wiser, and my career evolved with changes in government, I realised making money wasn't enough. I became frustrated when I worked hard for months, or even years, on something I believed in and knew would make a difference for good, only to see it undone or overturned the next time the governing party changed. I realised I wanted to make a real difference, not just go through the motions of changing things and then changing them back again, according to someone else's will.

When I raised the idea of starting a business with my parents (we are close, and discuss important decisions), they emphatically told me I shouldn't think any further about it, but I should stay in government employment. They reasoned I would always have a safe job there, and they saw it as the most financially stable option for me.

When I was in network marketing, I felt there was a big emphasis on earning money and the lifestyle and freedom money could bring. I was very attracted to earning money at the start, but I realised over time that while it would be nice to be wealthy, making a difference is much more important to me than stuff or lifestyle. I also learnt that while I certainly enjoy the freedom that running my own business gives me, it has many more responsibilities than I ever imagined.

I've also secretly dreamed for years of doing something on stage with a microphone in my hand; I always thought it would be singing. While I'm a reasonable singer and absolutely love singing my heart out on the worship team at church, I'm no professional, and I would certainly not like to have to sing for my supper! It never occurred to me, until I met a professional speaker on a cruise in 2014, that perhaps I could fulfil that dream by being a speaker.

But I forgot about my dream to be a speaker until I started my training to be a John C Maxwell Speaker, Trainer, and Coach. I loved my speaker training, and I picked up the skills quickly and easily because they made perfect sense to me.

Coaching came easily to me too. I had learnt to be an empathetic listener as a lawyer, and coaching took those skills a few steps further.

While I happily took on the job as a PR speaker for Guide Dogs NSW/ACT, I was reluctant to start speaking in my own right using my own material because I didn't feel like I had the authority or experience. Besides, why would anyone want to listen to me, and what would I talk about?

At the end of the cruise I mentioned in Chapter 3, I continued to work with my coach Regina. We unpacked the ideas I had discovered when examining my past, and I decided I wanted to work with people to help them discover their life's purpose and put it into action so they could lead happy and fulfilled lives.

Then I realised I really did have something worthwhile to say and I wanted to encourage larger groups of people through inspirational speaking. I had read, and been told, that to be a successful speaker, I would need to write a book, so I started writing my first book, coached a few clients, started recording a podcast, and forgot about speaking again.

Next, I was encouraged to attend a Christian Women in Business conference; however, I initially resisted because I usually prefer attending conferences with both men and women, and I didn't have the money anyway. But then someone had to pull out at the last minute and offered me their ticket at a very good price, so I decided to go.

During a number of sessions, we were encouraged to bring any issues we had in our businesses before God, and spend time waiting to hear a reply from him. As I waited, I felt that God was telling me very strongly to stop messing around and just speak! So, I decided I would.

Almost immediately, I was contacted by a complete stranger who had found me on LinkedIn. This person invited me to speak at a conference. But when COVID-19 hit, the conference was cancelled.

I knew I was meant to speak, so I started working with Kerrie Phipps, a well-established speaker and an excellent coach. Kerrie helped me overcome my limiting beliefs and refine my topics and messaging.

Then one of my podcast listeners contacted me to ask if I would speak to a group of people on a teleconference. When I did, I was surprised by the positive response. Soon after, I was contacted by another complete stranger on Facebook who invited me to speak to the Indian Forum of Educators via Zoom. My speaking career had begun!

EXERCISE: EXAMINING YOUR PASSIONS AND DREAMS

Do you have a passion you've put aside, or a dream you've squashed or forgotten about because:

- You don't think it is possible?
- You're not sure how to take the first step?
- You don't want to risk quitting your job, or outlaying a lot of money to make it possible?
- You've been discouraged to follow your passion or dream, or failed in your first attempt?

Regardless of whether you've put them aside or squashed them, take out your passions and dreams and take a good look at them. Perhaps one of them, in its current form, or a modified form, may be the very thing you have been put on this earth to do.

Write the answers to the following questions in the spaces provided.

1. What do you cry about, or what breaks your heart?

    _____

    _____

    _____

    _____

2. What makes you want to jump for joy, even just thinking about it?

    _____

    _____

    _____

    _____

3. What makes you feel so uncomfortable that you just have to do something about it?

    _____

    _____

    _____

    _____

4. What have you always wanted to do or be?

_____

_____

_____

_____

5. What do you daydream about when you have a spare minute, or when you're falling asleep at night?

_____

_____

_____

_____

6. What, if you did it every day, would cause you to wake up with excitement and enthusiasm?

_____

_____

_____

_____

7. What does, or could, drive you to do things, or work harder than you otherwise would?

_____

_____

_____

_____

It saddens me to think of the many people who are simply going through the motions of living because they don't know their life's purpose. It's almost as if they're marking time until they die! I was once like that, and I remember that empty feeling of lacking direction. I reacted to what happened to me, rather than taking intentional action to change my life for the better, or to set myself a direction.

What makes me literally sing for joy is knowing I've helped someone by encouraging, inspiring, or empowering them to change their life for the better and create a meaningful and fulfilling future for themselves.

Because I've always wanted to help people in some way, most of my daydreams have that theme running through them.

Working on anything to do with encouraging people to reach their full potential, such as speaking to a group, recording a podcast, or writing this book, gets me up in the morning, feeling excited and enthusiastic about what the day will bring.

This passion to encourage others gives me the strength to go on, despite failures and setbacks. It always lifts me up when I'm feeling down or having a bad day.

SUMMARY

Just like your present and your past, your passions and dreams can tell you a lot about yourself. Your passions can give you clues about what your purpose might be, and your dreams can give you clues about how you might like to put your life's purpose into action.

We all have passions and dreams. But many of us have forgotten about them or put them aside.

Our passions give us strong enthusiasm, and they keep us going when times are tough. Our dreams inspire us to believe and act.

CHAPTER 5

PUTTING YOUR LIFE'S PURPOSE INTO ACTION

"All you need is the plan, the road map, and the courage to press on to your destination."

— Earl Nightingale, American Speaker and Author

In Chapters 2, 3, and 4, I discussed the three steps you need to take to discover your life's purpose, and I shared the thought processes I went through and reverse-engineered to come up with these three steps. In this chapter, I will pull everything together to help you discover your life's purpose, and I will suggest ways you can figure out how to put it into action.

The processes of discovering your life's purpose and then figuring out how to put it into action don't necessarily have to occur in that order. The clients I have worked with have discovered their life's purpose first, and then they have decided how to put it into action, so that is how I've set out the processes in this book. However, that isn't how it worked for me. First, I discovered the how—speaking, coaching, and writing—and then stumbled across my life's purpose—inspiring and encouraging others to reach their full potential.

DISCOVERING YOUR LIFE'S PURPOSE

Discovering your life's purpose is like looking at the big picture. When I work with a client, I get them to examine their present, their past, and their passions and dreams. As they talk through their examinations with me, I will often notice a theme running through what they are saying. It might be a common word that keeps appearing, or a common concept. Usually when I point the theme out to the client, they are not surprised. We work on how to put the theme into a simple statement, much like working on a mission statement for an organisation, and that statement embodies the client's life's purpose.

As I said earlier, a life's purpose is usually a broad thing. Examples include to teach, to serve, to inspire and encourage others to reach their full potential, to heal, to provide opportunities, to create and grow leaders, etc.

In earlier chapters, I've told you about my process of discovering my life's purpose and how I decided to put it into action, so I won't repeat myself here. However, I will use what I discovered about myself to show how I would apply the process of discovering my life's purpose and putting it into action as if I were my own client, or a reader of this book. I will also illustrate how I applied the process to a few of my clients. (I've changed their names for privacy reasons.)

MY LIFE'S PURPOSE

When I examined my present the first time, I discovered the parts of my legal job I enjoyed most involved helping people find solutions to problems, writing, and giving training and presentations to my colleagues. I hadn't been happy in my job for a couple of years, and I felt undervalued and unappreciated by my supervisors and clients. Most importantly, I no longer felt I was making a difference.

When I examined my present the second time, I was finally able to admit I wasn't doing at all well in the network marketing business; in fact, I was losing more than I was making. The problem was I was unable or unwilling to follow the process to the letter.

When I examined my present the third time, I realised career coaching wasn't working for me. I wasn't able to get clients because I didn't feel authentically qualified to be a career coach.

My top interests were running a business, helping others, recording my voice, and speaking. My top skills were writing, speaking, and empathetic listening.

My top values were:

- Faith/creed/worship, i.e., expressing religious faith through commitment to its creed, teachings, and practices
- Congruence, i.e., walking the talk, authenticity
- Transformative communication, i.e., the desire to communicate transformative insights that change the way people live and view the world

Finally, my top personal quality was the ability to inspire and encourage others.

When I examined my past, I realised I had overcome many challenges. I seemed to have a knack for public speaking, and I had been drawn to it at various points of my life. I also seemed to be drawn to encouraging or helping others, and people said they found me inspiring and encouraging.

When I examined my passions and dreams, I realised it saddened me to think of the many people simply going through the motions of living because they don't know their purpose. I think I've always wanted to help people in some way, and most of my daydreams have that theme running through them.

The themes that run through my past, my present, and my passions and dreams are inspiring and encouraging others and public speaking. My life's purpose is to inspire and encourage others to reach their full potential.

KATHERINE'S LIFE'S PURPOSE

When I started working with Katherine, she was unhappy with her current life and was feeling restless. She wanted to discover her life's purpose because she wanted to return to study, but she didn't know what she wanted to study, or what she wanted to do with the rest of her life.

When Katherine examined her present, she felt her life was lacking purpose and direction. Katherine realised her superpowers were memory, self-deprecating humour, storytelling, research, problem solving, and listening.

Katherine didn't have the benefit of the CareerStorm Navigator tool or the values inventory, so I can't specifically write about her interests, skills, values, and personal qualities here.

When Katherine examined her past, she found she had been drawn to words, laughter, and being a generous listener.

When Katherine examined her passions and dreams, she realised she was passionate about fighting injustice, teaching, research, writing, and making people smile, being with others, travel and culture.

The themes that kept appearing for Katherine were writing, storytelling, and humour. We decided Katherine's life's purpose was to help people see things differently.

JUSTIN'S LIFE'S PURPOSE

When I started working with Justin, he was not happy in his government policy job. He wanted to discover his life's purpose so he could figure out what he wanted to do with the rest of his life.

When Justin examined his present, he felt he was too specialised in his field (security), and he wanted to broaden out a little. He didn't want to stay in a desk job; he wanted a job where he could move around more. He wanted a job that was more practical than theoretical.

Justin's superpowers were protecting, helping, risk management, and being calm in a crisis. Justin's top interests were risk management, security, psychology, sociology, and governance. His top skills were protecting, problem solving, applying information, analysing information, and assessing people. His top personal qualities were approachability and trustworthiness, being intellectually thoughtful and witty, being willing to help and serve, and being a straightforward communicator. Justin didn't have the benefit of the values inventory.

When Justin examined his past, he realised he was at his happiest when he wasn't tied to a desk and could move around a lot. Good working relationships with his colleagues were very important to him, and he loved doing anything related to security, risk management, and governance.

When Justin examined his passions and dreams, he realised the things that broke his heart were unrequited love, unfulfilled expectations in relationships, and the world's injustices. He was very uncomfortable with injustice and abuse of power.

Serving and caring for others and being in trusting and respectful relationships made him jump for joy.

Justin was passionate about caring for, protecting, and serving others, and he dreamt of being able to do something where he could see the practical effects of his work.

Justin realised he was passionate about the security field and risk management and governance, and he loved to learn and have variety in what he does.

The themes that kept coming up in our discussions centered on caring for others and security. We came to the conclusion that Justin's life's purpose was to serve, care for, and protect others.

JENNIFER'S LIFE'S PURPOSE

Earlier, I wrote about Jennifer's dream of being a musician. While I didn't work with her to discover her life's purpose, I did work with her using the CareerStorm Navigator tool to help her decide what she wanted to do after she took her severance package. While she didn't go through the exercises the other coaching clients did, it is not difficult to answer these questions based on information in the CareerStorm Navigator tool and the discussions I had with her for the purpose of writing her story in Chapter 1.

When I started working with Jennifer, she had just taken a severance package from the telecommunications company she had been working for because she found the pressure of work and feeling unappreciated by her supervisor were beginning to take a toll on her health. When I first spoke to Jennifer, she was deeply relieved she had left her job, but she was unsure what she wanted to do with the rest of her life.

Jennifer's top interests were communication, customer service, performing, singing, and developing resilience and confidence. Her top skills were performing, good memory, planning, cooperating, and decision-making. Her top personal qualities were being empathetic and caring, collaborative, highly motivated, always honest, and an attentive listener. I have heard Jennifer sing, and I can say without any doubt that singing is one of Jennifer's superpowers.

You will recall from Jennifer's earlier story that she had always had music in her past, and she had dreamt of being a professional musician.

Jennifer's life's purpose is to serve and bring joy to others through music and writing.

EXERCISE 1: WHAT IS YOUR LIFE'S PURPOSE?

In the space below, write out your life's purpose. You could write it in the form "My life's purpose is to _____

_____

" as my clients have, or "My life's purpose is to _____

_____

_____ so that _____ "

, as I have. It doesn't have to be right the first time. You can refine it over time.

PUTTING YOUR LIFE'S PURPOSE INTO ACTION

In Chapter 1, I described discovering your life's purpose as being similar to mining for and refining gold. Taking this analogy further, I believe that deciding how you will put your life's purpose into action is a little like deciding what to do with the refined gold. Gold is one of the most useful minerals mined from the earth; it is used in jewellery, as well as in coinage, electronics, computers, medicine, aerospace, glass making, awards, status symbols, and gold leaf and gilding.

Similarly, a life's purpose can be put into action in many ways. Sometimes, the client knows what they want to do as soon as they discover their life's purpose. Other times, the choice is more difficult and requires more self-examination, perhaps even some trial and error. Ultimately, the things you choose to do will be those that make your heart sing. They will be things you can do over and over, day after day, and never tire of doing.

Justin had no problem deciding how to put his life's purpose into action. After working with me, he left his policy job and obtained a more practical security job, in which he is very happy.

It also didn't take Katherine long to work out how she was going to put her life's purpose into action. After working with me, Katherine decided to write a book about her life as a person with a vision impairment. I suspect this is only the first step for her; she will undoubtedly find other ways to put her life's purpose into action. I look forward to seeing what she does.

As I said above, Jennifer wants to put her life's purpose into action through music and writing. I look forward to seeing how she refines this goal over time, and what she does.

I, on the other hand, had more difficulty deciding how to put my life's purpose into action. You will remember I tried career coaching and life's purpose coaching, and in early 2020, had recently pivoted into professional speaking. While I still intend to coach clients, I see speaking and podcasting as the primary ways I will put my life's purpose into action.

EXERCISE 2: PUTTING YOUR LIFE'S PURPOSE INTO ACTION

1. If you already know how you will put your purpose into action, write what you will do in the space below. Be as detailed as possible. You can skip the rest of this exercise.

   _____

   _____

   _____

   _____

If, like I did, you are having difficulty in deciding how to put your life's purpose into action, consider all the possible ways you could do this.

For example, if you discovered your life's purpose was to care for animals, you could put that purpose into action by becoming a veterinarian or veterinary nurse, a zookeeper, a carer for rescued wildlife, a foster carer for animals needing rehoming, a dog walker, a horse whisperer, a dog groomer, a volunteer at an animal shelter, etc. You could work to raise funds to care for animals, or even just donate money on a regular basis.

2. In the space below, list all the ways you could put your life's purpose into action. Don't exercise any judgement at this stage; just list all the possibilities.

_____

_____

_____

_____

3. Look at your list above, and put a tick next to all the possibilities that make you feel happy.

_____

_____

_____

_____

4. Now, consider the possibilities you have not ticked. If you didn't
    tick a possibility just because the thought of it scared you, tick
    it. Rub out or cross out any remaining unticked possibilities.

_____

_____

_____

_____

5. For each of the possibilities you ticked, find out all you can
    about each one, including qualifications required and the cost
    of obtaining them, potential income that can be earned, what
    you will be doing on a daily basis, whether you might need to
    change the location where you live, etc.

_____

_____

_____

_____

Once you know how you will put your life's purpose into action,
you will need to decide whether you will put it into action as a ca-

reer or as a hobby. In making this decision, you will need to take into account the information you gained above.

Returning to the animal carer example above, all these options require different levels of training, and they have different levels of responsibility attached. Some can be done as a full-time career or hobby, and some require very little time or effort.

You could work with a coach, like I did, to go through the various options of how you could put your life's purpose into action. Day-dream—let your mind wander and experience what a day in the life of you will be like. This process gets easier and details become clearer the more you do it.

You could even write a story from your future self to your current self. This will show up any gaps that can often stem from doubts or fears or plain lack of knowledge. As you come across more details, add them to your story.

TESTING AND REFINING

As you become clearer about your life's purpose and how you will put it into action, it will become like a dream for the future. But before you rush off and start living your dream, it's important to put it to the test to see if it is possible.

In his book *Put Your Dream to the Test*, John C Maxwell defines a dream as:

"an inspiring picture of the future that energises your mind, will and emotions, empowering you to do everything you can to achieve it. A genuine dream is a picture and blueprint of a person's purpose and potential."

Maxwell suggests ten questions to ask yourself about your dream:

1. Is your dream really your dream, or someone else's?

2. Do you clearly see your dream?

3. Are you depending on factors within your control to achieve your dream?

4. Does your dream compel you to follow it?

5. Do you have a strategy to reach your dream?

6. Have you included the people you need to achieve your dream?

7. Are you willing to pay the price for your dream?

8. Are you moving closer to your dream?

9. Does working towards your dream bring satisfaction?

10. Does your dream benefit others?

The more of these questions you can answer with a definite "yes", the more likely you will be to achieve your dream of putting your life's purpose into action.

Don't be discouraged if you don't get everything right the first time around. You may need to refine the wording of your life's purpose slightly. More likely, though, you will need to refine how you put your life's purpose into action. I certainly have. I don't regret any of the time spent, or the mistakes I've made along the way because I've learnt a great deal about myself, much of which I've put into this book. I only hope what I've learnt on my journey will help you on yours.

SUMMARY

In this chapter, I have pulled together the thought processes I detailed in previous chapters to reveal my life's purpose. I have also shared how a number of my coaching clients have gone through this process to discover theirs.

The processes of discovering your life's purpose and then figuring out how to put it into action don't necessarily have to occur in that order. Discovering your life's purpose is like looking at the big picture and finding a theme that runs through your present, your past, and your passions and dreams. Your life's purpose is a broad thing.

Deciding how to put your life's purpose into action is a little like deciding what to do with gold once it has been mined and refined. Just as gold has many possible uses, often many choices exist for how to put your life's purpose into action. You may need to research various options to choose the right one.

Once you have decided how to put your life's purpose into action, you will need to decide whether you will do it as a career or as a hobby. You will need to take into account factors that include qualifications required, potential income, location, duties, etc.

As you get clearer about your life's purpose and how to put it into action, it will become like a dream. You will need to put this dream to the test to see if it is possible.

Refining your life's purpose and how you will put it into action may take time. However, the time taken and mistakes made along the way are well worth it because you will learn a great deal about yourself, as I have.

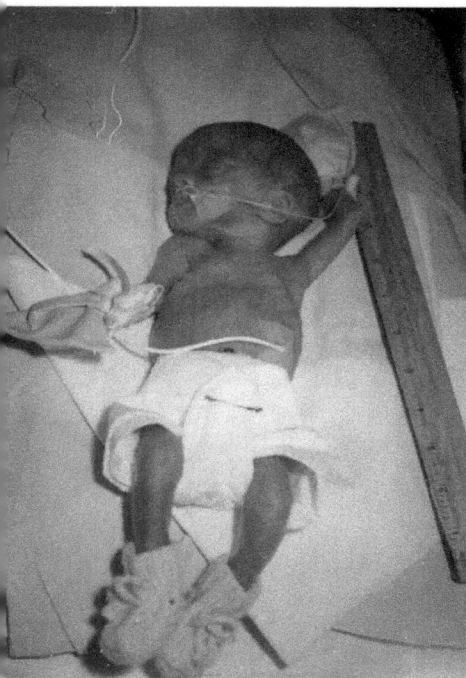
Amanda at 8 days old, March 1970

Amanda and Father Michael mowing the lawn, 1973

School photo 1976

Amanda playing trumpet, accompanied by music teacher, Ross

Amanda receiving commerce degree
with guide dog Gypsy, April 1994

Amanda receiving law degree
with guide dog Pebbles, April 1996

Amanda, Glenn, Ched, and Marjorie washing elephant

Amanda, Ed, Marjorie, and
Wangchuk patting baby rhino

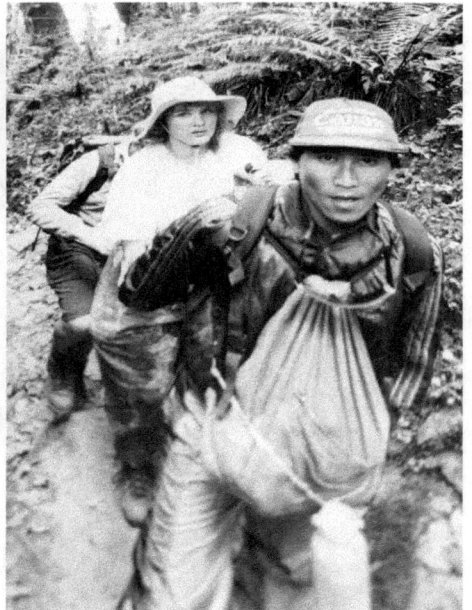
Amanda trekking in Nepal with sherpa guide

Carnival Legend at anchor

Amanda and Mother Valmai
meeting the captain aboard Carnival Legend

Amanda and Mother Valmai enjoying champagne aboard Carnival Splendour

Amanda and Mother Valmai under Christmas
tree aboard Carnival Splendour

Amanda and Mother Valmai
on training walk for Nepal Trek

Whole trekking group at summit of Poon Hill (altitude 3,210M, 10,531 ft)

Raft going through rough rapids

Raft going through rough rapids

Amanda Heal speaking on stage

PART II

THE TOOLS YOU WILL NEED ALONG THE WAY

"Give me six hours to chop down a tree and I will spend the first four sharpening the axe."

— Abraham Lincoln, Sixteenth President of the United States

CHAPTER 6

FINDING COURAGE
IS THE KEY

"Man cannot discover new oceans unless he has
the courage to lose sight of the shore."

— Andre Gide, French Author and Winner
of the Nobel Prize in Literature

In Part I of this book, I discussed how to discover your life's purpose and put it into action. In Part II, I will provide some of the tools you will need to do that. In this chapter, I will discuss the importance of courage in the process of discovering your life's purpose and putting it into action.

WHAT IS COURAGE?

Courage has been described as many things by different people:

- "a kind of salvation" — Greek philosopher Plato
- "a perfect sensibility of the measure of danger and the mental willingness to endure it" — US General William Tecumseh Sherman
- "resistance to fear, mastery of fear, not absence of fear" — American writer Mark Twain
- "the capacity to confront what can be imagined" — American writer Leo Rosten
- "never to let your actions be influenced by your fears" — Hungarian British author and journalist Arthur Koestler

I used to think courage was the absence of fear, but as many of the definitions show, courage is not the absence of fear, but deciding to do something despite the fear.

Throughout my life as a blind person, people have often told me I'm courageous. I'd think to myself, "Well, no, I'm just living my life". I could never understand why anyone would think of me as courageous. It took me many years to learn that courage is a subjective thing, and it is different for different people. What some people think of as courageous, other people think of as perfectly normal.

In 1992, I was privileged to be asked to join a group of vision-impaired people to go trekking in Nepal. This trek was organised by Guide Dogs NSW/ACT to enable a group of people of different ages and with different levels of vision to improve their confidence and mobility skills, promote the association, and show that blind and vision-impaired people like to enjoy the same sorts of activities as their sighted peers.

Eight of us were in the group. The vision-impaired contingent consisted of Ched Towns (now deceased) and his brother John, Ed Holicky, Narelle Head, Marjorie Roberts (now deceased), and myself. We also had two sighted people in the group—Glenn Butterworth and his friend Jon Gettoes. We were also accompanied by a film crew who would film the trek.

When I was first invited to go on the expedition, I was a little hesitant. I knew nothing about Nepal except that Mount Everest was there, and I didn't think I was up to climbing that! But after talking with Glenn about where we would be going and who else would be in the group, I decided it sounded fun.

We were an eclectic mix of people. Glenn was the Public Relations Manager for Guide Dogs NSW/ACT, and the trek was his idea. Glenn and John spent most of their spare time trekking and rock climbing together, and Jon was coming on the trip as photographer to take photos of our adventure.

Ched was a triathlete who had successfully completed an Ironman triathlon. Ed was also an athlete, who had competed in the 400m sprint in the 1992 Barcelona Paralympic Games.

Marjorie was in her sixties and had recently lost her vision due to a brain haemorrhage. She was fiercely independent and wasn't going to let anything stop her, not even her sudden vision loss.

Narelle and Ched's brother John only had eyes for one another, so I never got to know either of them well before or during the trek.

I was the youngest in the group and halfway through my combined commerce/law degree. The trek had come at an ideal time for me because I was bored with the monotony of study and needed a bit of adventure.

Ched and I were the only guide dog users in the group. The others used long canes or had enough vision to get around reasonably safely without any mobility aids. Ched and I could not take our guide dogs to Nepal, and it would be very difficult for us all to navigate the Annapurna Foothills in Nepal using long canes. The plan was that we would each be matched up with a Sherpa who would guide us over the mountainous terrain.

We had all grown up in towns and cities, so we were used to travelling on footpaths with our guide dogs or long canes. To prepare, we went on a number of walks in national parks so we could experience different surfaces and experiment with different methods of being guided by Jon, Glenn, and the family members who came with us.

My parents owned a caravan by the sea, and my mum and I had perfected a safe way to explore the rocks and beaches together. When we were walking on flat sand, I'd hold onto her elbow and walk half a step behind her, the standard way of guiding a blind person. But when we came to rocks, I'd walk behind her and hold onto her hips. That way, I could feel which leg she was moving, and where she was putting her feet, so I could walk directly in her footsteps. This technique needed to be modified for the many ups and downs of a mountain trail, so we experimented walking together with me holding onto a backpack Mum was carrying, and it worked.

When I showed this technique to the others in the group, some were unimpressed because they felt they had enough vision to be guided using a trekking pole with their guide holding onto one end and them holding the other. But by the time we left for Nepal, they were all holding their guides' backpacks like me.

While I can't speak for the others in the group, I was very grateful for all those training walks we did and for the experience I had gained walking with Mum across the rocks since some parts of the trek were very difficult. While I was holding onto my guide's backpack, he still needed to give me verbal instructions as to where to put my feet such as "Step up and over the tree root", or "Be careful, the mud is slippery here". Because I was the only totally blind person in the group and needed more instruction than the others, Glenn or our head guide, Wangchuk, would often guide me to give my guide a break.

Our Sherpa guides were absolutely wonderful. They guided us safely for twelve days up to an altitude of 3,210M (1,0531ft) and down again. At the highest point of our trek, Poon Hill, Wangchuk took each of us by the hand and pointed our hands to the major mountains he could see—Dhaulagiri, Annapurna I, II, and III, etc. Of course, we all wanted to know where Mount Everest was. Wangchuk explained he couldn't see it from where we were, but he showed us what direction it was in.

Despite our guides' diligence and care, we still had quite a few slips and trips along the way. Someone, I can't remember who, decided we should have a competition. The person who had the most "technical falls" would have to buy the others a drink at the end of the trek. A "technical fall" would be defined as a fall where three points of the faller's body would touch the ground, e.g., two knees and a hand. Some debate ensued as to whether two butt cheeks counted as two separate body parts, and we eventually decided they would. The Sherpas quickly got in on the act, and you would often hear a Sherpa voice call down the trail "Technical fall!". I think we decided Glenn was the winner because he managed to fall down a steep drop, touching the ground with his entire body. Thankfully, he only twisted his ankle slightly and was back in action again after a rest day.

The local people would often ask us why we were trekking in Nepal when we couldn't see the views. Wangchuk would always tell them we could "see Nepal through the eyes of our soul". I never quite knew what that meant, but it seemed to make them happy.

I may not have been able to see the views, but I loved all the sounds, smells, textures, and even tastes I experienced, and I loved meeting the local people as we trekked. Having never seen mountains before, I thought they were all cone-shaped. During the rest day, Glenn made a plasticine model of one of the mountains he could see, and I was fascinated by the irregular shape of it, and all the ridges and buttresses it had.

From conversations I had with the other group members, I learnt that for some of them, it had taken courage to go on the trip. Marjorie was still dealing with the grief of her recent vision loss and finding the balance between being independent and relying on others for help when she needed it. Ched and his wife had been together since he was a teenager, and they were virtually inseparable. He became tearful one day as he told us how much he missed her since she had not come with us on the trek; he had become very dependent on her as his vision got steadily worse.

Personally, the only times I had to draw on my courage were when we went through some grade-four rapids during a day of white-water rafting, and when, in Chitwan National Park, I got to sit on an elephant's neck as it stood up.

For some of us, I don't think courage really entered our minds that often during the trip. This was a wonderful adventure and an experience we would never forget. I can understand, though, why sighted people would think we were courageous trekking through Nepal guided by complete strangers, some of whom didn't speak a great deal of English, white water rafting, and washing and riding elephants.

WHY IS COURAGE IMPORTANT?

Many times exist when, during the process of discovering your life's purpose and putting it into action, you might need courage. I've certainly needed it.

When I was facing the prospect of being laid off, it took courage to look outside the box of government employment to consider other options. My parents had both been employed by the government when I was young, and they had always told me that government employment was the best option for me. In some ways, this was true because the government had equal employment opportunity policies in place to make it easier for people with disabilities to enter into and remain in government employment. Back when I started working for the government, it was much easier to get access to expensive adaptive equipment than it was in the private sector. So, I had firmly intrenched beliefs about the safety of government employment, and the possible dangers of private sector employment.

When I was considering going into network marketing as a hobby or side hustle, it didn't require much courage because I had done it before, and it was never something I depended upon for my major source of income. However, seriously considering network marketing as a possible full-time job was completely different. What would happen if I couldn't sell anything or get anyone to join my business? Could I live on my severance payout and superannuation? These questions raised all sorts of fears around security and wealth because if I didn't do well in network marketing, I would have to live on half the income I had earned in my government employment, meaning I would have to make some big lifestyle changes.

In Chapter 2, I told you of how I fell and very seriously injured my knee, and that I had spent two months recovering in a splint. During my recovery, I had the time to look back over the past year. I realised I had not been happy for some time because I was losing more money than I was making, and I felt frustrated that my business was not growing. I had worked so hard to convince myself and others that I could be successful that I hadn't been able to bring myself to admit I had been wrong and it was time to make a change. I think the trauma of my injury and my long recovery was the wakeup call I needed to face my own fear of admitting failure and the fear that everyone around me would say, "I told you so; now go back and get a proper job". Thankfully, no one did.

I had two options: return to paid work, or retrain as a John C Maxwell speaker and coach. I had been out of work for a year and couldn't face the thought of going back to a nine to five job. Retraining as a speaker and coach meant I could continue being self-employed, but it would require me to invest a substantial portion of my savings into the training, and to take a week-long trip to America to get certified.

I needed to find the courage to believe in myself and my training when I started coaching clients. I was consumed with fears that I wouldn't be able to help them, and that they wouldn't be willing to pay me for my services. When I eventually decided once and for all to become a speaker in my own right, and when I started writing my first book, I had to overcome the fear that people wouldn't buy my book or book me to speak because I didn't have anything worthy to say.

Most importantly, it took courage to let go of my limiting beliefs, some old habits, and my past careers and the identities they gave me. I needed to let go of these because they were limiting my ability to truly search for my life's purpose.

EXERCISE 1: YOUR FEARS

Hopefully, you are now some way on the journey to discovering your life's purpose. Write the answers to the questions below in the space provided.

1. What are all the things you have encountered along the way toward discovering your life's purpose and putting it into action that have caused you to feel fear?

    _____

    _____

    _____

    _____

    _____

2. Are any of those things holding you back from discovering your life's purpose or putting it into action? How?

    _____

    _____

    _____

    _____

    _____

COURAGE REQUIRES YOU TO FACE YOUR FEARS

As a totally blind person, I've faced a number of fears, and I can offer three tips to face and overcome them.

1. **Figure out where the fear sits on the catastrophe scale.**

    The catastrophe scale is used by children and adults to put fear into perspective. At the top of the scale are catastrophic things like the death of a loved one, and at the bottom are mere annoyances. Everything else fits in the middle. Another way to put fear in perspective is to look at the severity of the consequences of the thing you fear occurring.

    About six months after I started my network marketing business, I decided I wanted to attend the company's Global Training Conference in Las Vegas. I was convinced I would learn there what I needed to do to make my failing business more successful. I learnt a lot, but not what I was expecting.

    I was hoping to travel to Las Vegas with people I knew, but I couldn't afford to take an extended holiday as the others were doing. So, if I wanted to attend the conference, I would have to travel there and back on my own.

    I had travelled domestically and internationally on my own before, but I had never had to change planes, and I was always met at my destination by someone I knew and trusted. This trip would require me to change planes twice and then get to the MGM Grand on my own. Once there, I would have to figure out how to find the other Australians there I knew because I would need their help to get around the massive hotel and to and from the conference venue.

What scared me most about this journey was the possibility of getting lost. My parents freely voiced their fears for my safety, which didn't help!

As I get older and wiser, I'm beginning to realise that getting lost isn't as catastrophic as I might think. I can usually ask someone for help or call someone to come and rescue me. But international travel adds another layer of consequences, such as missed flights and increased risk of danger by being in unfamiliar places surrounded by strangers. So, for me, the consequences of getting lost were fairly severe.

2. **Calculate the likelihood of the thing you fear occurring.**

If you know how likely it is that the thing you fear will occur, you can weigh it against the consequences of the thing you fear in a sort of risk analysis. Conducting this analysis can help put things in perspective and lower your level of fear.

If I were to travel on my own without any pre-travel preparation, the likelihood of me getting lost was extremely high. I was not familiar with the airports I would have to travel to, and I would have to rely on the kindness of fellow passengers for help.

3. **Work out what can be done to lessen the severity of the consequences of the thing you fear occurring or lessen the likelihood of it occurring.**

I decided if I was going to make this trip, I would have to prepare. Thankfully, I found a wonderful travel agent at Flight Centre who quickly understood my needs and got to work. He contacted the airlines and let them know I would need assistance on and off each flight and assistance to get from one flight to the next. The shorthand for this in the airline industry is "meet and assist". He also contacted the MGM Grand to let them know a blind guest would be checking in on a particular date.

For my part, I arranged for a friend to drive me to the airport and take me to the check-in counter for my airline. There I was met by a staff member who took me to the airline lounge, and then on to the flight. I carried a long cane with me that I unfolded whenever I was left alone in an airline lounge or departure gate so I would be visible for the next staff member who would need to collect me, and I made sure when boarding each flight that the cabin crew knew I would need "meet and assist" at the other end.

Finally, when I got to Las Vegas, I asked the staff member who took me off my flight to take me to a taxi, which she did. I told the driver where I wanted to go, and I made sure when he dropped me at the MGM Grand that he didn't leave until I had been greeted by the concierge and taken inside. Someone from reception took me to my room and gave me the number to dial reception if I needed anything. Then it was just a quick message on Facebook, and I was in contact with my friends who had already checked in.

All the preparation was worth it. The journeys were safe and uneventful, and I had a wonderful time at the conference. I now know I can travel anywhere in the world I like.

EXERCISE 2: ANALYSING YOUR FEARS

For each of the fears listed in Exercise 1, and any others you can think of, answer the following questions.

1. Where does the fear sit on the catastrophe scale, or alternatively, what are the consequences of the thing you fear occurring?

_____

_____

_____

_____

2. What is the risk of the thing you fear occurring?

_____

_____

_____

_____

3. What can you do to lessen the risk of the thing you fear occurring, or lessen the severity of the consequences if the thing you fear occurs?

_____

_____

_____

_____

COURAGE REQUIRES CONVICTION

In his podcast, Nick Vujicic says one thing you need to build and maintain courage is conviction. Nick was born without arms and legs; no one knows why.

When Nick was eleven, he told his little brother he was going to commit suicide when he turned twenty-one because he felt a man with no limbs could not hold down a job, marry, or provide for a family, so he would be no use to society. Of course, his brother told his father, who comforted Nick and told him they would work everything out somehow. Everything would be okay.

Nick didn't commit suicide. He got married and had four children. And now he travels the world as a speaker. Nick was able to do these things because of the conviction he had of the love of his family. He knew his family couldn't give him arms and legs. But he knew they loved him, and that gave him the courage to keep going.

The two things that keep me going are my life's purpose and my faith.

EXERCISE 3: YOUR CONVICTIONS

What convictions do you have that could help give you courage? They could include things like the love of your family, your faith, or even your life's purpose if you've discovered it already.

_____

_____

_____

_____

COURAGE REQUIRES SETTING GOALS AND BREAKING THEM DOWN INTO BITE-SIZED PIECES

Teacher and psychologist Richard Snyder conducted a long-term study into the effect of hope on students' academic success. He found that the best-performing students were able to create clear and meaningful goals, had the willpower to succeed, and were able to create strategies to achieve their goals.

I believe the same applies to courage. If we set clear and meaningful goals, we know where we are heading and are much more likely to succeed. As we experience small wins in life, such as achieving steps towards a larger goal, our belief in ourselves grows. And as we become more confident in achieving bigger goals, it leads to greater belief in ourselves and greater courage.

In Chapter 3, I told you how I had dreamt of being a speaker, and how I had been invited to be a public relations speaker for Guide Dogs NSW/ACT. But I almost gave up on that dream because of my fear of catching buses.

When I was asked, at the interview, how I would get to and from the various schools and other organisations where I would speak, I responded, "By taxi, of course, like any other self-respecting speaker who can't drive".

When I was told I would be expected to get to as many of the venues as possible using public transport, I panicked and nearly threw up in the interviewer's lap! I hadn't caught a bus on my own in more than twenty years, and I had become so afraid of the prospect of travelling alone on a bus that even the sound of a bus going past would make my heart race. I firmly believed if I caught a bus on my own, I would get lost, and it absolutely terrified me.

I had just finished reading John C Maxwell's book *Everyone Communicates, Few Connect*, in which he said that to be an authentic communicator, you have to live the message you are communicating. It made sense to me, then, that I couldn't talk to people about traveling independently with a guide dog if I wasn't doing that myself. Also, I really wanted the job. So, I agreed to undertake two weeks of intensive training to learn how to travel on buses again.

Because my anxiety was so great, I had to start small—just getting on and off a stationary bus and finding a seat. While getting on and off the bus didn't worry me, I was anxious because I thought perhaps I was taking too long to find a seat, and the bus would take off, causing me to lose my balance. But when I talked to the off-duty bus driver about this, she explained that, in Canberra, bus drivers are trained to wait until elderly or blind passengers sit down before taking off. We finished this first step with the driver driving round the block, and me practicing locating and ringing the bell and getting off and back on the bus.

Once I was comfortable with this process, I went on a short bus journey with a guide dog instructor sitting beside me and keeping me calm. Next, I travelled on the same journey with the instructor somewhere on the bus (I didn't know where) in case something went wrong. Finally, I travelled alone on the bus and met the instructor at an agreed location.

Being able to break down my goal of independent bus travel enabled me to achieve each step, which built my confidence enough for me to progress on to the next step. It was all worth it. I didn't get lost, I conquered my fears of bus travel, and I now travel all over Canberra by bus to speak.

EXERCISE 4: YOUR GOALS

1. What are some goals you can set to help you discover your life's purpose or put it into action?

    _____

    _____

    _____

    _____

    _____

    _____

    _____

2. For each goal, write down the bite-sized pieces you can break it
    down into to make it easier to achieve.

_____

_____

_____

_____

_____

_____

_____

COURAGE REQUIRES PRACTICE

In her book *Brave*, Margie Warrell says if you take action despite
your fears, you'll become a stronger person. She says that every time
you face your fears, you'll be strengthening your courage muscles.

Before the coronavirus struck, I was travelling by bus to different
venues once or twice a month. My confidence grew until I was
calm enough to take out my phone and check my email during the
bus journey.

But after the virus struck, all face-to-face talks were cancelled for about four months. When I went back to speaking, that first bus journey wasn't easy because I had lost quite a bit of confidence over those four months of not catching buses. It made me aware that bus travel will probably be one of those things I just have to keep practicing to keep my courage up and my anxiety down.

Others have described courage as being like a habit. To form a habit, it is necessary to repeat a certain behaviour over and over until it becomes normal. Margie Warrell suggests we can develop the habit of courage by practicing small acts of courage on a regular basis.

Thinking back over the last few years, I've been doing a bit of this myself. Each time I've tried, failed, and tried again to finally learn a new skill—such as making decent-looking videos for social media, experimenting with marketing a new coaching package, or writing and rehearsing a new speech for a new audience—I've had to bring a little bit of courage to the process. Each time, I've drawn courage from my past wins to help me progress on to the next one. Each time, I've been willing to step up and try something a little harder or a little bigger.

EXERCISE 5: ACTS OF COURAGE

You can do many small things to practice getting outside your comfort zone and building your courage, such as driving a new route to work, speaking up or asking a question in a meeting when you'd usually not do so, or talking to a stranger. The task doesn't have to terrify you, just make you a little uncomfortable.

In the space below, write down some things you could do to build your courage.

_____

_____

_____

_____

_____

_____

_____

_____

_____

_____

SUMMARY

Courage means different things to different people. It is not the absence of fear but deciding to do something despite the fear.

Courage is important because it allows us to face the fears and limiting beliefs that may be preventing us from discovering our life's purpose and putting it into action.

Courage requires us to face our fears and overcome them. You can do this by rating the thing you fear on the catastrophe scale, calculating its risk, and working out what to do to lessen the risk or the severity of the consequences of the thing you fear occurring.

Courage requires conviction, which helps us face our fears. Courage requires us to set goals and break them down into smaller pieces so we can build our confidence and self-belief as we achieve them. Courage also requires practice, which helps us build our courage muscle and get stronger.

CHAPTER 7

DEALING WITH CHANGE

"The only way to make sense out of change is to plunge into it, move with it, and join the dance."

— Alan Watts, British Writer and Speaker

In Chapter 6, I discussed the first tool I believe you need to discover your life's purpose and put it into action: courage. In this chapter, I will discuss the second: dealing with change.

In researching this topic, I found a lot written about how to impose a change upon ourselves; e.g., giving up smoking or losing weight. A lot has also been written about how to manage the imposition of change upon others, such as managing employees undergoing a change in organisational structure. However, I couldn't find much about how to deal with change when we have little or no control over what is happening to us. That's the sort of change I will be dealing with in this chapter.

In his book *Life Without Limits*, Nick Vujicic tells of how his parents decided to move from Australia to the US when he was a child. He had no control over the decision to move because he was a child. Nick had been popular at his school in Australia, and he was very happy there. All the students and teachers there had come to terms with his lack of limbs and treated him normally.

But when he had to start school in the US, he found things very difficult. Initially, his teachers didn't treat him like everyone else, and the students found him strange. Eventually, he was able to make friends and adjust.

On 19 May 2018 at around 10.30pm, my phone rang. "Daddy's dead!" my mum screamed into the phone. My father had not been well for years, and his health had recently deteriorated more quickly, but Mum had not expected to find him dead in his bed that night. They had known each other for fifty-four years and been married for fifty of those.

Initially, Mum was shocked and numb, but as the weeks went by, she began to grieve. Mum seemed to lose most of her ability to make decisions, particularly important ones, without support from her family. She also lost the confidence to do things she had done previously, such as driving and socialising on her own.

But as the months went by, Mum slowly began to adapt. Dad had always done all the work outside the house, so Mum had to learn how to start the lawn mower, operate a chainsaw, and use an electric drill. She's now quite proficient at all of these. She was worried about her finances, so I eventually convinced her to sign up for online banking so she could see where her money was and where it was going. She now happily transfers money between her accounts and pays bills, all using her iPhone. She also regularly attends her local seniors' club, both in person, and via Zoom.

WHY IS EMBRACING CHANGE IMPORTANT?

When you discover your life's purpose and put it into action, you may face a number of changes. Some of those changes you will have control over, such as changing your job or the way you spend your leisure time. Other changes may be unexpected, such as changes in self-confidence, and others may be changes you have little or no control over, such as the reactions of those close to you. Because my journey to discover my life's purpose and put it into action wasn't planned, many of the changes I had to deal with were unexpected, and some I had no control over. But as I went along, more of the changes were those I chose to make.

I was surprised just how much I was affected by my loss of identity when I left my legal job and started my network marketing business. For seventeen years, whenever anyone asked me what I did, I would say, "I'm a lawyer", and for the last seven of those years, I took quite some pride in saying, "I'm a legislative drafter". So, after I left my legal job and started selling skin care products, I didn't know what to say when people would ask me what I did. I couldn't really say I was a lawyer because I didn't have a practicing certificate. I had never needed to get one because I was included under the practicing certificate of the senior lawyer in each government department I worked in. I didn't really feel comfortable saying I was a skincare consultant because I was still learning about the products and hadn't made many sales.

Then there was the change from being an employee to owning my own business. I had been an employee all of my life, and I always knew if I were unable to do my job due to illness or being off work for some other reason such as a holiday, someone else would do the work.

I always had someone senior to me at work, so the buck never stopped with me as far as decision making. It was quite a shock to realise that as a business owner, when I didn't do the work, it didn't get done, and I didn't earn money. If I was having difficulty making a decision, there were certainly people I could turn to for advice, but ultimately, the buck stopped with me. My business' success or failure was entirely up to me.

I hadn't expected the diversity in my friends and family member's reactions to my decision to take a severance package and sell skincare products via network marketing. Some fully expected me to remain in paid legal work, thinking self-employment was just a passing phase, and they continued to send me advertisements for legal jobs until I begged them to stop. Others expressed their dismay of how I could "waste all that time becoming a lawyer and throw it all away", and they persisted in telling others I was still a lawyer.

Others were supportive to varying degrees. Some hosted workshops for me and they still buy products from me. Others purchased from me once and then never again. A few don't talk to me anymore, due to my overzealous and persistent sales and recruiting promotions.

As far as my mindset went, it was a bit like being on a rollercoaster. Throughout the process of being laid off, I was plagued with feelings of rejection and depression. When I started my network marketing business, I experienced feelings of relief, as well as belonging and acceptance. Each time I'd hold a workshop with good sales, I'd feel elated, as if I were on my way to conquering the world. But when workshops didn't bring in good sales, I'd experience doubt and disappointment, and I would feel resentful towards those who were succeeding.

In my network marketing business, I had to work hard to overcome limiting beliefs such as: I don't know enough about the products, I don't know enough people to make this work, and I'm too old. As I moved into coaching and speaking, I had to work harder still to overcome beliefs, such as I'm not good enough to do this, no one will listen to what I have to say, I don't have enough experience, and no one will pay me.

THREE STEPS TO EMBRACING CHANGE

One of the most difficult and painful changes I have to go through every eight to ten years or so is retiring my current guide dog and taking on another one. Currently, I am on my fourth guide dog, Sadie, and I can honestly say the process of changing guide dogs never gets any easier. While I have some control over this change, with many parts of it, I have no control at all.

Many people think when someone is working with a guide dog, they just pick up the harness handle and the dog takes them where they need to go. This is not true. Guide dogs are trained to walk in a straight line, avoid obstacles, stop when they encounter steps or curbs, and target destinations such as doorways, counters, and seats. The dogs can also learn the names of particular destinations such as the doorway to a particular chemist or a particular bakery counter, and they will find these when they are close by.

So, for example, if I want to go to the chemist from my home, I still have to give Sadie directions all the way along the route for when to turn left or right or to cross roads. I only say "find the chemist" when I know we are getting close to the chemist's doorway. Sadie's job is to keep me safe along the way by ensuring I don't run into obstacles or people and I don't fall up or down stairs or trip over curbs. Some have compared the intelligence of a guide dog to that of a small child.

Sadie and I are very much a team, and as you can probably imagine, we have a very strong bond. She is not only my best friend, but I literally trust her with my safety, and even my life.

Each time I've retired a guide dog and taken on a new one, I've had to form that strong bond again and develop the trust necessary for us to work as a team. This is very hard.

Because I've gone through this process three times now, I have come up with three steps I use to help embrace this change, and change in general.

1. Prepare for the change.

I believe that before you go through a major change, it is essential to prepare for that change the best you can. Learn as much as you can about the change—what it will involve, how it will occur, the consequences that will arise from it, etc.

I didn't know much about my previous three guide dogs before I met them. However, Sadie was sponsored by a pet food company, and there was quite a bit about her on social media. So, I was able to read stories about her, and have photos described to me before we met.

Sometimes, people have the opportunity to go on a trial walk with their prospective new dog. I wasn't able to do this because I was planning to be overseas when Sadie completed her training. So, I had a long talk with her trainer to find out as much as possible about her personality and the way she had been trained.

I was also able to get in touch with Sadie's puppy raiser, the person who raised Sadie from the time she left the Guide Dog Centre at six weeks of age, until she started her guide dog training at around twelve months old. I was able to find out all about her history as a puppy, her likes and dislikes, her favourite toys, the sort of mischief she could get up to, etc.

2.   Create space for the change.

Another thing essential in embracing a major change is to create space for it. This could involve letting go of how things were before the change in order to create space and acceptance for how they will be after the change. It could also involve forgiving those responsible for the change, if it is imposed on you, or perhaps forgiving yourself for things that happened in the past that may have led to the change occurring. It may also involve dealing with any grief that may come up during this step.

Every time I change guide dogs, I have to let go of the past. Training methods change over time, and the techniques used to work with the dog also change. So, each time, I have to be willing to let go of what I knew and take on something new.

When I retired my first two dogs, Gypsy and Pebbles, I experienced a certain amount of grief, mainly because our working relationship was ending. Fortunately, I was still able to see them both regularly because they went to live with my parents, whom I would see a few times a week. I was working full-time at that stage, so it would have been unkind to make them adjust to being home alone eight hours a day.

When I decided, along with the guide dog instructors, that I should retire one of my dogs soon, my name would be put on the waiting list for a new dog. I was fortunate to be able to work Gypsy right up until I got Pebbles, and work Pebbles right up until I got Gillies.

The changeover from Gillies to Sadie was much harder. Gillies developed a slipped disk in his lower spine, which initially caused him a lot of pain. When we got this under control, he gradually lost the strength in his back legs and was unable to walk any distance. He stayed with me after he retired because I was no longer working full-time and could keep him company during the day. But after twelve months, he could hardly walk at all, so I made the heartbreaking decision to have him put to sleep.

A couple of months after Gillies' back got bad, I had the serious knee injury I mentioned in Chapter 2. I had put my name down on the waiting list for a new dog, but it had to be taken off the list until I was fit enough to train and work with one.

Not only did I have to learn to walk again, but I had to relearn how to walk with a long cane so I could move around independently outside my home and get stronger in preparation for getting a new dog. Walking with a long cane is very different to walking with a guide dog. When I walk with a long cane, I hold the cane's handle in one hand and slide the tip in a shoulder-width arc along the ground. I have to time the arcs of the cane with my steps. Walking with a guide dog is much more natural because I just hold the harness handle and walk. So, I found going back to using the long cane very unpleasant. I would go so far as to say it made me feel disabled. But it was something I had to do if I wanted to be independent and to get my fitness back so I could get my new dog.

I was fortunate to be in a TV ad for Guide Dogs NSW/ACT in 1992. When the ad's creator, Ray Hall, asked me what having a guide dog meant to me, I tried to explain the difference between walking with a guide dog and walking with a long cane. He expressed this so beautifully in the song used in the ad that I want to include the first verse here:

> I never found the time to smell the flowers,
> I never found the time to hear the birds,
> I was concentrating hard where I was going,
> I listened but I never really heard.
> But now I've found the time to smell the flowers,
> Time to listen to the song of life,
> Time to stop and taste a summer shower
> For you've brought something special to my life,
> You've helped me see the world through different eyes.

When I got Sadie, I was still dealing with the grief of Gillies' death since he had only died just over a month before. I also had to forgive myself for the decisions I'd made regarding the amount and duration of treatment for his back.

Another thing I had to let go of was the trauma of my knee injury the year before. While I had recovered completely from the physical injury, I would still have the occasional flashback of falling, and I was still very hesitant around steps. I had to learn to trust Sadie to do her job and not let me fall down steps. Dear Sadie picked up on my hesitancy through the harness handle almost immediately, and even now, years later, she is still very careful not to take me close to the edges of steps. After a couple of weeks working with Sadie, my flashbacks disappeared and have never returned.

3. Accept and commit.

Finally, it is necessary to accept the change and commit to it wholeheartedly. Just accepting the change isn't enough because, without committing to it, it's too easy to want to go back to the old way of doing things when it gets hard.

Every time I get a new dog, I have to commit to that dog 100 percent. I need to put everything I have into forming a strong bond with the dog and trusting the dog so we can work well together.

EXERCISE

1. List all the changes that might occur during the process of discovering your life's purpose and putting it into action.

    _____

    _____

    _____

    _____

    _____

2. For each change listed above, list all the things you know about that change. Is there anything you need to find out more about?

_____

_____

_____

_____

3. For each change above, list the things you will need to let go of, and any possible sources of grief.

_____

_____

_____

_____

4. For each change, list all the things you will need to accept and commit to wholeheartedly.

_____

_____

_____

_____

_____

SUMMARY

Embracing change is important because you may face many changes whilst discovering your life's purpose and putting it into action. These may include changes in others' reactions, changes in mindset, and changes in circumstances.

My recommended three steps to embrace change are to prepare for the change, create space for the change, and accept and commit wholeheartedly to the change.

CHAPTER 8

LEARNING TO LEAD

"I am the master of my fate, I am the captain of my soul."

— William Ernest Henley, Poet

I n Chapter 7, I discussed the second tool I believe you need to discover your purpose and put it into action—embracing change. In this chapter, I will discuss the third—leadership.

When we think of leadership, most of us think of leading others. I certainly did. But a very valuable lesson I learnt during my network marketing days is that before you can lead others, you must first be able to lead yourself, and that is what this chapter is about.

WHAT IS SELF-LEADERSHIP?

Professor Charles E Manz is believed to be the first person to use the term "self-leadership". He defined it in 1983 as "a comprehensive self-influence perspective that concerns leading oneself". Management consultant, educator, and author Peter Drucker said that being a self-leader is to serve as chief, captain, or CEO of one's own life. Andrew Bryant and Anna Kazan, in their book *Self-Leadership: How to Become a More Successful, Efficient, and Effective Leader from the Inside Out*, define self-leadership as "the practice of intentionally influencing your thinking, feeling and actions towards your objective/s".

WHY IS SELF-LEADERSHIP IMPORTANT?

I believe that, for most of us, our life's purpose is bigger than we are. Therefore, to put our life's purpose into action, we need to grow into it.

John C Maxwell puts this very well:

> If you want to reach your full potential and become the person you were created to be, you must do much more than just experience life and hope that you learn what you need along the way. You must go out of your way to seize growth opportunities as if your future depended on it. Why? Because it does.

Growth doesn't just happen—not for me, not for you, not for anybody. You HAVE TO go after it.

MY PERSONAL GROWTH JOURNEY

I know I've been learning and growing since the day I was born. At times, my learning and growth were intentional, such as when I was studying at university or attending professional development and continuing legal education courses whilst working as a lawyer. But I can honestly say my learning and growth weren't self-led until I started my network marketing business.

I knew that to have a successful network marketing business, I had to do two things: sell product and recruit others into my business. So, I rapidly became the stereotypical network marketing person everyone hates. I talked about nothing but my business, what a wonderful lifestyle change it was, and how happy it was making me. I pushed my products onto people at every possible opportunity, relentlessly emailing my friends and family and posting on social media about the products.

While I didn't recruit anyone or make many sales, I continued on, believing it was just a matter of time. I didn't realise anything was wrong with my strategy until two things happened. Firstly, I got an angry reply from an ex-colleague to one of my sales emails. She pointed out that I had never asked her how she was or what she was doing, but just tried to sell her something, so could I please remove her name from my contact list. Secondly, I was about to start a conversation with a friend at a restaurant when my dad called out across the table "Don't let her con you into buying anything".

At about this time, I met Wendy, another consultant in my business whom I mentioned in Chapter 2. She taught me that to lead others, I first had to learn to lead myself. She also taught me that leadership is all about influence. So, I did all I could to learn about leadership—reading books, participating in Wendy's leadership masterminds, and practicing my leadership skills by teaching and leading others in Project Starfish America (more about that later).

As I studied leadership, I began to see areas in my own life that were lacking, particularly my mindset and attitude to success. I could not possibly hope to influence others until I sorted these out. So, I went out of my way to find mentors (face to face, online, and in books) who could teach me what I needed to know. I also did some self-actualisation work through the personal and professional growth organisations The Institute for Self-Actualisation and Landmark.

As I put what I was learning into practice, I gradually began to change. I began to realise success wasn't just about how much money I could earn; it was about how I felt within myself, how I treated others, and most importantly, living in accordance with my values and beliefs and being a living example to others. I realised I couldn't rely on anyone else for my happiness or success; I was entirely responsible for both.

Wendy observed how the leadership training was changing my life and invited me to join the John Maxwell team to become a Certified John C Maxwell Speaker, Teacher, Trainer, and Coach. I spent the next three months completing the intensive online training before traveling to the US to obtain my certification.

However, my personal growth journey didn't end there. I wrote earlier about how I gained clarity around my life's purpose and would put it into action, and the various coaches and clients I've been privileged to work with. As I pivoted from coaching into professional speaking, I've continued with more focused personal development. I don't think I'll ever stop learning.

NASREEN'S STORY

I've never seen anyone grow as much as my dear friend Nasreen. But before I tell you her story, I need to tell you a little about Project Starfish America and its founder, Subhashish Acharya ("Subs"). Subs was born in Calcutta, India. He has always had a place for blind people in his heart because his family owned a number of eye hospitals and he has had a number of blind friends since childhood.

Subs studied engineering, but he got into developing internet video games. That came to an abrupt halt after the September 11 terrorist attacks. He lost everything and became homeless.

Fortunately, a friend saw potential in Subs and gave him the opportunity to work for a local IT company. Subs then realised the one thing that prevented many people from attaining success was opportunity. Subs worked his way up in the company, and eventually transferred to Oracle. Oracle gave him the opportunity to move to the US with his wife.

Years later, Subs attended a job fair for the blind. He was struck by the number of companies that were there just for show and had no intention of offering employment to any of the blind attendees. He thought there must be a better way for blind people to obtain employment.

In 2013, Subs and his wife founded Project Starfish America, a unique way for blind people to find employment. Candidates are interviewed to assess their suitability, and if accepted, they start learning about how a business works by going through case studies with Subs. I was one of these candidates. I joined Project Starfish America just before I left my legal job in 2014.

Once I and the other candidates had a reasonable understanding of how different businesses worked, Subs would arrange for us all to get on a conference call with a small business he had researched and contacted on behalf of Project Starfish America. We would listen to the business owner tell the story of what the business did and how it had been formed. Subs would then ask the business owner about problems they were having in the daily running of the business, and invariably, the business owner would tell us they needed extra help. Because most of us were professionals who had not been able to find work, or who had become unemployed, we had skills to offer these small business owners such as customer service and research. We offered our skills for a small fee or for free to a business. The idea was the business would get the help it needed, and we would get the experience we needed to gain employment with that or another business.

A few months after I joined Project Starfish America, Nasreen came on board. My first impression of her was she had little to say and little confidence in herself. But as the months went by, that began to change.

Nasreen had not been blind all her life. In fact, she didn't start to lose her sight until she became pregnant with her daughter. Before her pregnancy, Nasreen had worked in a number of different jobs, including in a factory and doing administrative and retail jobs. During her pregnancy, Nasreen was working in a bookshop, but she eventually resigned because she felt she could no longer do her job due to her deteriorating vision.

Nasreen was told her vision would likely return to normal after she gave birth, but it didn't. About two years after her daughter was born, Nasreen was diagnosed with retinitis pigmentosa, an eye condition which causes loss of peripheral vision, and in some cas-es, total blindness.

As her vision deteriorated, Nasreen took a lot of online classes to learn how to use adaptive technology for the blind. During these classes, Nasreen came across a number of blind people who didn't seem to have any goals or practical skills, but they had much more potential than they gave themselves credit for. A desire started to grow in Nasreen to help these people discover their full potential and to teach them the practical skills needed to find employment. This desire ended up being her life's purpose.

When Nasreen joined Project Starfish America, she told Subs about her life's purpose. Subs immediately saw the potential in Nasreen and asked her to teach everyone in Project Starfish America how to use Microsoft Word to create documents of sufficient standard and quality for business use. She agreed.

Nasreen's Microsoft Word course was a hit. Subs then got all the members together and asked us what we were able to teach since we all had different skills in different areas. I was good at using Mi-crosoft Outlook, so I volunteered to teach that. Others agreed to teach Twitter, LinkedIn, Microsoft Excel, sales, research, etc. We all taught each other what we knew, and then we combined our knowledge into a training program all new candidates would have to go through before they could get on calls with business owners and work on projects with businesses.

Nasreen was rarely absent from case study calls or calls with business owners, and she was absorbing information like a sponge. As her confidence and skills grew, Subs encouraged her to interact more with the business owners. She eventually took over moderating the calls, pitching our skills to businesses, and organising projects with them. It seemed the more responsibility Nasreen was given, the more she thrived, and the more she wanted to take on.

Nasreen was very good at reading people, so she took over the process of interviewing candidates for Project Starfish America. This work wasn't for everyone. Those who joined had to be self-motivated and willing to work hard for very little pay in order to learn and gain experience.

By this time, I had joined the John Maxwell Team, so Subs asked me to run some leadership and personal development masterminds for the other members. Needless to say, Nasreen was always the first to sign up for these, and she was an enthusiastic participant. She didn't just absorb knowledge; she applied it to her work and daily life.

Nasreen began to work more and more closely with Subs, and she rose to each challenge he gave her. She began to see each challenge not as something to be feared, but as an obstacle to be overcome, and she found this thrilling. If something needed to be done and Nasreen didn't know how, she'd research the process thoroughly, improve upon what she found, and implement her improved process in Project Starfish America.

Subs eventually appointed Nasreen as CEO of Project Starfish America. He had been promoted himself, so he was spending less and less time working with us. A number of people in India were interested in joining us, so Nasreen spent a great deal of time training and growing the members in India, and eventually, she trained one of the members in India to lead that team. Since losing her sight, Nasreen had not travelled independently outside her home, but after joining Project Starfish America, she twice overcame her fears to travel alone to India.

Nasreen has now expanded Project Starfish America to work not just with blind people, but with sighted veterans and their spouses, sighted students, and even people being released from prison. She has also formed a partnership with the Sourcing Institute so that blind people can be trained to be recruiters and talent sourcers.

I've been privileged to watch Nasreen grow from what she was when I first met her into what she is today. Nasreen's growth was not by chance; it was focused and very much guided by her, so she could put her life's purpose into action, as she is doing today.

EXERCISE 1: LEADING YOUR PERSONAL GROWTH

1. In the space below, copy your life's purpose from Chapter 5.

_____

_____

_____

_____

_____

2. Return to Chapter 2 and look at your skills and personal qual-
    ities in Exercises 3 and 5. Are there any skills or personal qual-
    ities not on those lists that you will need to grow into your life's
    purpose and put it into action? List them below, and then rank
    them in order of importance.

_____

_____

_____

_____

3. What actions do you need to take to learn these skills and at-
    tain these personal qualities? Actions could include reading
    particular books, doing certain courses, or asking particular
    people to help or mentor you. List the actions below, and then
    rank them in order of importance, according to your answers
    to question 2. Don't worry if you can't think of them all. More
    will come to you over time, and you will be able to delete some

of them from the list as better alternatives emerge.

SELF-DISCIPLINE

I'll be honest; personal growth is not always easy, and it requires self-discipline. I've never really been particularly good at self-discipline, but I do well with any type of learning and particularly personal growth.

One reason many of us fail at self-discipline is we don't have sufficient motivation to do whatever we're trying to discipline ourselves to do. I'm very good at short-term diets to lose weight for a particular event, but I'm really bad at sticking to long-term weight loss because I just don't care enough. My enjoyment of the good things in life outweighs my desire to weigh less.

On the other hand, I was very good at getting my assignments done at school and university because I was terrified of failure. I also didn't want to disappoint my parents, particularly my father, who expected me to do well. These motivations were sufficient to keep me going day after day, year after year.

Today, however, the thing that motivates me most is my life's purpose. I'm always eager to learn anything that will make me a better person or improve my skills so I can better inspire and encourage others. Now that I have my life's purpose to motivate me, personal growth is easy.

Another reason many of us fail at self-discipline is we don't make whatever we're trying to do into a routine or habit. I want to read the Bible every day, but I have found it very difficult to make it into a habit. I've tried all sorts of things, such as setting daily reminders and using various reading plans alone and with others, but none have worked for me long term. What seems to work best for me is to ask my smart speaker to read one chapter of the Bible to me each day when I'm having breakfast. Breakfast is part of my daily routine, which I never skip, so it's easy to listen to my speaker read to me while I eat.

Another thing that can trip us up is trying to start with a goal that is too big. In Chapter 6, I wrote about how I had the opportunity to go trekking in Nepal. At that time, I was a university student and not particularly fit. I was determined I would not be the person huffing and puffing at the back of the trekking group, and I knew I had six months to get fit. So, I started small, exercising on an exercise bike for five minutes. Each day, I would increase my exercise time by two minutes. Eventually, I was exercising on a StairMaster for one hour, twice a day, with a heavy pack on my back. If I'd started off my fitness campaign by exercising for one hour each day, with a view to building up to two, I would have given up very quickly because it would have been much too hard for me.

The final reason we fail at self-discipline is a lack of consistency. It's so easy to miss a day, get behind, or just give up. When it comes to personal growth, I think consistency in commitment is more important than consistency in the amount we do. It's very easy to say "I'm too busy" or "I don't have time", but if we just commit to doing one thing each day on personal growth, whether it is one hour of learning, or reading one page of a book, the commitment itself is enough to keep us going.

EXERCISE 2: SELF-DISCIPLINE

1.   How often will you commit to doing some sort of personal growth activity, and how much time are you willing to spend on that activity?

_____

_____

_____

_____

2. What systems or reminders could you put in place to help you be consistent?

_____

_____

_____

_____

SUMMARY

When most people think of leadership, they think of leading others. But before you can lead others, you need to be able to lead yourself.

Self-leadership is intentionally leading yourself.

Self-leadership is important because, for most of us, our life's purpose is bigger than we are. So, to discover our life's purpose and put it into action, we need to lead our own growth into it.

Personal growth is not always easy, and it requires self-discipline. And self-discipline requires sufficient motivation, ways to form habits, and consistency.

CHAPTER 9

MASTERING YOUR MINDSET

"Nothing in life has any meaning except the meaning we give it."

— Tony Robbins, Speaker and Author

I n Chapter 8, I discussed self-leadership, particularly in relation to personal growth. In this chapter, I will discuss another tool I believe is vital to discovering your purpose and putting it into action—mastering your mindset.

WHY IS MASTERING YOUR MINDSET IMPORTANT?

The *Macquarie Dictionary* defines mindset as "a particular mental framework of attitudes, expectations, prejudices, etc".

These attitudes, expectations, and prejudices live in our subconscious mind. They are like a filter through which we live life.

Our emotions come from our conscious mind, and they affect our decision-making and behaviour. Our conscious mind is affected by our subconscious mind, which means our mindset affects everything we do.

The problem here is our subconscious mind is not rational or reasoning. It just accepts what is put into it, and reacts accordingly. For example, all my life I've believed sharks are dangerous and I should be afraid of them. I associate the music from the movie *Jaws* with sharks. So, whenever I hear that music, I feel slightly anxious. My conscious mind knows it's just music, that *Jaws* is a movie, and that I'm not in the water with a shark. But my subconscious mind still affects my emotions.

The positive side to this situation is we can free our subconscious mind in a way that can, over time, change our mindset. Scientists call this neuroplasticity.

OVERCOMING LIMITING BELIEFS

One of the most important mindsets to overcome is limiting beliefs.

The *Macquarie Dictionary* defines a belief as "that which is believed; an accepted opinion; conviction of the truth or reality of a thing, based upon grounds insufficient to afford positive knowledge…".

Some examples of limiting beliefs include:

1. I've specialised, so I can't possibly do anything else.
2. All my family have done this, so I have to as well.
3. I'm too old or too young.
4. It has always been this way, and so it must continue.
5. This happened to me as a child, so it will continue to happen to me as an adult.

I've had to overcome a number of limiting beliefs, and I have watched others do the same. Based on these experiences, I've come up with four steps I believe can help us overcome our limiting beliefs.

1.   Recognise the belief is a limiting belief.

One of the most crippling limiting beliefs I've had is the belief I couldn't catch buses, which I referred to earlier in this book. I believed if I caught a bus on my own, I would get lost, and that would be catastrophic.

In Chapter 8, I wrote about Nasreen and her amazing personal growth from unemployed to CEO of Project Starfish America. When Nasreen was appointed as CEO of Project Starfish America, she firmly believed she couldn't possibly be CEO. When she told me this, I was puzzled because I knew her duties hadn't changed at all, just her job title. But after a lot of talking, we realised that deep down, Nasreen believed an Asian woman, who had only worked in factories and retail, and then as a mother, couldn't possibly be good enough to be a CEO.

The easiest way to recognise a limiting belief is to see that belief's consequences, i.e., what it is stopping us from doing. My belief that I couldn't catch buses was preventing me from travelling independently. While this wasn't a big deal most of the time, I missed out on doing some things simply because I couldn't get to where they were. Also, when I was offered the job as PR speaker for Guide Dogs NSW/ACT, I was expected to be able to travel independently as much as possible; not catching buses would mean I wasn't able to do that.

Nasreen's belief that she couldn't be CEO with her background and lack of experience temporarily stopped her from stepping into that role. While she had been performing the duties of CEO for months, the thought of taking on the title brought her to a standstill.

We often back up our limiting beliefs with excuses such as "I don't know the bus timetables" or "I don't have any experience as a CEO". Bus timetables are accessible online and through iPhone apps. Everyone who steps into their first CEO role lacks experience working under that title, but they will often have the necessary practical skills to do the job.

2. Decide whether the limiting belief is important enough to make the effort to overcome it.

Most of the time when I didn't catch buses, everything was fine. I could usually get a lift to where I wanted to go, or pay for a taxi. However, when I was offered the job as Public Relations Speaker for Guide Dogs NSW/ACT, traveling by public transport was one condition of the job. This job was very important to me so I agreed to overcome my belief that I couldn't catch buses by doing some intensive training.

In Nasreen's case, she had a company to run. She loved the work she was doing, and it was very important to her. The founder, Subs, had been promoted in his day job, so he no longer had time to spend on the day-to-day running of the company. So, Nasreen also overcame her limiting belief.

3. Question the truth, reality, and origin of the belief.

Some limiting beliefs are just untrue. Some originate from things that have happened in the past that are no longer relevant. Some beliefs are based on family or cultural traditions. The truth of some can be revealed through research or by just putting them to the test.

I had caught buses to school and university in the past, so my limiting belief had originated from not having caught a bus in almost twenty years and completely losing my confidence. The belief I would get lost was untrue because I had never got lost in the past when I had caught buses, and plenty of other blind people were catching buses, trains, trams, etc., every day without any problems. Once I regained my confidence, I was able to catch buses again.

When I was a child, no one ever wanted me on their team for sports or games. I was very bad at sports so I couldn't blame them, but it didn't do my self-esteem any good to regularly hear "Do I have to have her on my team?" I quickly formed the belief that no one would ever want me on their team.

But very recently, I attended a conference where we had a night of fancy dress, fun, and games. When the team games started, I immediately said I'd sit them out. Much to my surprise, the other attendees encouraged me to play and even picked me for their team! They happily helped me when I needed it, and we even won some of the games. I put the truth of that belief to the test and proved it wrong.

In Nasreen's case, she had been performing the duties of a CEO for months. The only thing that had changed was her job title. So, in truth, she had the experience and skills required to be the CEO. She put her belief that she was not good enough to the test, and she is still proving it wrong today.

4. Defeat it!

One way to defeat a limiting belief is to find alternatives to the belief. Here are the beliefs I listed at the beginning of this section with possible alternatives:

Limiting Belief	Alternative
I've specialised, so can't possibly do anything else.	My skills are, in fact, transferrable.
All my family have done this, so I have to as well.	I am my own person and don't have to be bound by family tradition or culture.
I'm too old or too young.	Unless there's a law that states otherwise, age is irrelevant.

Limiting Belief	Alternative
It has always been this way, and so it must continue.	Perhaps it's time for a change.
This happened to me as a child, so it will continue to happen to me as an adult.	Children can be cruel, but adults usually have more compassion and understanding.

Another way to defeat a limiting belief is by using positive affirmations. If I ever find myself getting anxious on a bus, I just tell myself, "I know where I am; everything is okay". When I was being bullied by a particular supervisor, I would spend my trip into work telling myself I really was good at my job, so I didn't deserve to be bullied.

If you are a person of faith, as I am, you could look up scripture to refute your limiting belief. Alternatively, you could pray or meditate.

Finally, you could just feel the fear and do it anyway. That is the only way to defeat some limiting beliefs. It is mainly how Nasreen defeated her limiting belief.

EXERCISE 1: OVERCOMING YOUR LIMITING BELIEFS

1. In the space below, list all the limiting beliefs you are aware of.

    _____

    _____

    _____

    _____

    _____

2. Is there anything you are afraid to do that wasn't covered in question 1? Could this fear stem from a limiting belief? List your fears below. If you can connect these to any limiting beliefs, add them to the list in question 1.

    _____

    _____

    _____

    _____

    _____

3. For each belief listed in question 1, rank it according to how important it is to put in the effort to overcome it. You could use a scale where 1 is not at all important, and 5 is extremely important.

    _____

    _____

    _____

    _____

4. For any beliefs you ranked 3 or above in question 3, where do those beliefs come from? Can you question their truth or reality? Can you overcome them with research, or can you put them to the test?

    _____

    _____

    _____

    _____

5. For any beliefs you ranked 3 or above in question 3, can you defeat them by finding alternatives, by using positive affirmations, or through faith? If all of these fail, are you willing to face your fears and defeat that belief?

_____

_____

_____

_____

OVERCOMING LONELINESS

You may not think of loneliness as a mindset, but it can be. It is possible to feel lonely when we're surrounded by people. Also, the extent to which we are affected by loneliness can be inherited, and loneliness in childhood can lead to loneliness in adulthood.

Loneliness isn't just a problem that magically appeared with the coronavirus. It has been around forever.

Loneliness is a feeling of sadness or distress about being by our-selves or feeling disconnected from the world around us. Putting it another way, loneliness is that negative feeling that arises when our social needs are unmet by the quantity and quality of our current social relationships.

A 2018 national survey of Americans aged forty-five and over showed that one third of adults were affected by loneliness, and a 2018 study in the UK showed that loneliness was most common in the 15-25 age group.

It's not just humans who experience loneliness. A news article reported that when zoos were closed due to the coronavirus, many animals were missing their interactions with the public. Some were even still turning up at their appointed visiting times. Some keepers were having lunch with their animals to keep them company.

The journey towards discovering your life's purpose can sometimes feel very lonely. It is your life's purpose, no one else's, and sometimes it feels like no one understands what you're doing or why.

When I left my legal job and started my network marketing business, many times I felt lonely and misunderstood. The transition from employee to small business owner was a bit of a shock because I could no longer walk into the next office and ask for help, and the buck stopped with me.

One of the best ways I've found to overcome this type of loneliness is to keep busy. One of the worst things about loneliness is it can leave a great deal of room for negative self-talk in our heads. When I felt particularly lonely after leaving work, I'd sit and list all the things wrong with my life—business not going well, very few friends, not getting out much, etc., and I'd get into a downward spiral where I'd become more and more miserable. But, if I could find something else to focus on, those thoughts would be crowded out and go away.

When I couldn't find a work task or hobby to keep me busy, I'd turn to an audio book—usually epic fantasy—to keep my mind active.

Another thing that helps a lot is to find people you can talk to who understand what you're doing. Perhaps find other people who are on a similar journey of discovery, or if you've discovered your life's purpose and are putting it into action, find people doing something similar.

Since pivoting into speaking, I've joined a speaker community. I love spending time with the other speakers, learning, sharing information, and swapping stories. I'm also in a number of small business communities, which I find very helpful and supportive.

Researchers are finding that spiritual beliefs and practices can be effective in combating loneliness. As I get better at practicing my faith, it becomes easier for me to feel God's presence—I just have to reach out to him and he is there, like a friend in the same room. Similarly, as I get better at listening to him, my conversations with him are becoming more two-sided than one way. But that's just me—we all have our own journeys in that respect.

I rarely have trouble with loneliness these days because I'm very clear on what my life's purpose is and how I'm putting it into action. Once you get clarity on these things, any loneliness you experienced in the past will almost all go away because your mind will rarely have time to go off on negative adventures of its own.

BUILDING AND MAINTAINING HOPE

The *Oxford English Dictionary* defines hope as: "A feeling of expectation and desire for a particular thing to happen".

Shane J Lopez, in his book *Making Hope Happen*, says hope is like oxygen; we can't live without it. Studies conducted by Lopez and his colleagues show that hope leads to everything from better performance in school and more success in the workplace to greater happiness overall. According to Lopez, "When we're excited about what's next", we invest more in our daily lives, and we can see beyond current challenges.

Hope gets us through bad times. World War II Polish resistance hero Witold Pilecki had a very strong hope that Poland would one day be free. When he was young, he joined the Polish resistance movement. Hope got him through his time in the Auschwitz concentration camp, where he helped to smuggle food and medicine into the camp and maintain contact with the outside world. He was the first person to let the Allies know what was really going on in the camp.

After World War II, Pilecki fought against communist forces. He was imprisoned and tortured for a number of years before being executed, and I have no doubt that hope got him through that time as well. Just before he died, Pilecki said he could die with joy in his heart because he knew he had done everything he could to help his people.

In Chapter 6, I discussed how courage can be built by setting meaningful goals and breaking them down into bite-sized pieces. The same applies to hope. If we set clear and meaningful goals, we know where we are heading, so we are much more likely to succeed. As we experience small wins in life, such as achieving steps towards a larger goal, our belief grows and we become more confident in achieving bigger goals, leading to more belief and greater hope. If we have multiple strategies to achieve our goals, it further increases our chances of success.

In Chapter 6, I told you how I regained my confidence to catch buses again and how I got fit for my Nepal trek by breaking down these big goals into smaller, more achievable pieces, and how that led to my success.

Another way to build and maintain hope is to surround yourself with the right people. As motivational speaker Jim Rohn famously said, "We are the average of the five people we spend the most time with".

If you are going to build and maintain your hope, you need people around you who will support you, lift you up when you are down, and even push you a little. You need to spend as little time as possible with people who are negative, or who don't support you in achieving your goals.

If you are surrounding yourself with family or loved ones, be aware that they may not be able to push you as much as you might need.

That is because they love you and naturally want to protect you from anything they may perceive as harmful, such as you making mistakes or even failing.

The people you surround yourself with don't even have to be people you personally know. They can be people in books or even movies. I love to read books about people who inspire and encourage me. I find that I learn so much from them.

EXERCISE 2: BUILDING AND MAINTAINING YOUR HOPE

1. In the space below, write down the names of all the people you admire, or who inspire you, whether they be fictitious or real.

    _____

    _____

    _____

2. List the books you could read or movies you could watch to learn about and from these people.

    _____

    _____

    _____

BUILDING GRATITUDE

One very important mindset to have is gratitude. Neuroscientist Dr Caroline Leaf says when we are grateful, our brains release neurotransmitters and neurohormones that will boost mood, focus, and clear thinking, and that will enhance mental energy and physical health.

Shortly after I started my network marketing business, I complained to one of my mentors that everyone else was having success except me. I expected her to come up with a list of solutions to my problem, but instead, she told me I needed to learn to be more grateful because in my current state of mind, I was driving people away from me and my business, rather than attracting them. She challenged me to think of one thing every day for a month that I could be grateful for.

I took up the challenge, and it has been life-changing. My mindset gradually changed from being negative to being positive. I began to think more creatively, and solutions to problems popped into my head far more often than they used to. Even now, years later, I am able to see the positive in situations far more readily than I ever could before. I think this change has made me into a happier and more successful person.

My attitude of gratitude had some unexpected consequences. In Chapter 6, I told you about my trip to a conference in Las Vegas.

When I checked out of my room after the conference, I had about six hours to kill before I flew back to Australia. I had arranged to hang out by the pool with a friend, but plans changed at the last minute, so she couldn't make it.

I couldn't think of what else to do, so I went to reception and asked where I could sit for a while. When I explained to them that I had a six-hour wait ahead of me, they very kindly took me to their VIP lounge so I could be more comfortable.

I sat in the lounge, feeling disappointed and frustrated that I had to be there with no one to talk to for six hours. Then I remembered my gratitude challenge. As I pondered what I could be grateful for, I realised I was sitting on a very comfortable seat, which was much more comfortable than any of the seats in the cafes nearby, so I was grateful for that. I checked my phone and realised I had free Wi-Fi, so I was grateful for that too. Starting to feel quite happy about the situation, I put my headphones on and started to watch self-development videos.

Then, someone tapped me on the shoulder and said hello. It was the CEO of the network company. She had seen the company's logo on the bag at my feet and come over to see who I was. Never in a million years did I think I would get to talk to the CEO of such a big company, so I was absolutely thrilled. I told her that meeting her would make the next six hours in the lounge worth it, and she left.

A little later, she returned and said she'd arranged, at the company's expense, for me to have something to eat before I left. I was very grateful, and I thanked her, thinking she meant someone would bring me food in the lounge.

I was extremely surprised when the head butler of the MGM Grand came and took me up to the penthouse for a meal. To top it all off, he suggested that instead of travelling to the airport in a taxi, I should go in one of the MGM Grand's cars. I gratefully accepted, having no idea that the car he spoke of was a Rolls-Royce! I felt like a princess!

As we glided to the airport in the most comfortable car I've ever travelled in, I reflected on the afternoon's events. If I hadn't changed my attitude from miserable to grateful, I probably would have had a sour look on my face and the CEO wouldn't have given me a second look. I wouldn't have met her, and I wouldn't have enjoyed being treated like a princess for the afternoon. So, I've come to firmly believe an attitude of gratitude really can attract blessings.

SUMMARY

Mastering mindset is vital because our subconscious mental framework of attitudes, expectations, prejudices, etc. has a direct effect on our emotions and actions.

Overcome limiting beliefs by recognising them, deciding they are important enough to overcome, questioning their validity and origin, and defeating them with alternatives. Build hope by setting goals and getting support from others. Overcome loneliness by keeping busy and focusing on purpose. Exercise gratitude to stay healthy and focused, and perhaps even attract some blessings.

CHAPTER 10

MANAGING YOUR FINANCES

"Don't let making a living prevent you from making a life."

— John Wooden, American Basketball Player and Coach

In Chapter 9, I discussed the importance of mindset. In this chapter, I will discuss the importance of managing your finances based on my own experiences and research. While I am not a qualified financial adviser, this chapter has been reviewed by one.

WHY IS MANAGING YOUR FINANCES IMPORTANT?

Managing your finances while discovering your life's purpose and putting it into action is important for numerous reasons:

- Costs may be associated with discovering your life's purpose and putting it into action such as retraining, relocation, etc. (see Chapter 5).

- If you are considering changing jobs, the bigger the savings buffer you have, the better because you may not be able to walk into another job immediately.

- If you are considering putting your life's purpose into action by running a business, startup costs will be involved, and the less you need to go into debt to cover those costs, the better.

- You may find the income you earn through putting your life's purpose into action is permanently less than your current income, or that it will take some time to build it up to what you are currently earning.

WORKING OUT YOUR CURRENT AND FUTURE FINANCIAL POSITION

Before you make any decisions that will affect your finances, it is important to take a snapshot of your financial position. It you have a really good idea of exactly what income you have, and where it goes, you are in a much better position to figure out the consequences of any changes to your income. The simplest way to figure out those consequences is to ask yourself, "What do I have, and what do I need?" Then work out the consequences of any decision you make based on that financial position.

When the agency I worked for was downsized in 2014 and I was unsuccessful in reapplying for my job, I had a choice. I could:

1. Take a package and leave immediately.

2. Continue working for the agency for six months and take whatever employment I could get during that time.

3. Continue working for the agency for six months, and get a severance package of around half of what I would get if I left immediately.

A job freeze was on at the time, so options 2 and 3 were not attractive. But before I made a decision, I had to find out all I could about my current financial position.

To make sure I didn't miss anything, I went through all my bank statements and bills for the past year. I calculated all my income and expenses down to the cent, and then I averaged them out over the year. This gave me figures for my average monthly income and average monthly expenses. I was in a very good financial position because I was earning more than I was spending each month, and I was accumulating savings. I had more than I needed.

If I decided to leave my employment immediately, I knew the money I received would go a long way towards paying off my mortgage. But because my income would be around half of what I was earning, I wouldn't be able to maintain my current level of monthly expenses, unless I dipped into my savings, which I preferred not to do.

So, I looked more closely at my expenses to see what I could eliminate. I was surprised to realise just how much I was spending without even realising it. I was paying for a number of membership and app subscriptions I hadn't used for months or even years. Also, when I had changed my gym membership from one location to another, my first membership hadn't been cancelled, so I was paying twice for the same membership! I was also shocked to realise just how much unnecessary stuff I was buying online, just because I could.

I realised that if I cut out all those expenses and decreased my leisure and holiday expenses slightly, I could decrease my monthly expenses enough that I could live on my reduced income.

As mentioned earlier, I had decided to start a network marketing business and sell skin care products. Thankfully, the startup costs were low; I only needed to purchase some catalogues, some forms, and the products to show clients, and I could use most of these products myself day to day. Also, I didn't have to keep extra product at home because customers' orders were shipped directly to them from the warehouse. The one thing I didn't know was how much I would earn from this business.

So, I decided to take the severance package and leave my employment immediately. If I was careful, I would be able to live on my reduced income, and any income I earned from my network marketing business would be a bonus.

SEEKING PROFESSIONAL ADVICE

Before I go any further with this chapter, I must stress how important it is to seek professional financial advice before you make any decisions that could substantially affect your finances. So many things must be considered, such as tax, superannuation, various bank fees and charges, investment strategies, etc. If you are thinking of starting a business, you will also have to consider such things as business structure, registration, licensing requirements, business financing, insurance, and health and safety. So, you should seek financial and even legal advice.

Once I had a good idea of my current and future financial position, I went to see a financial adviser. They were able to advise me on the superannuation and tax implications of taking a severance package, how much I should put into the mortgage, and how much I should invest. We also discussed the pros and cons of different additional sources of income, some of which I will discuss below.

I didn't need to obtain legal advice because I was advised by my network marketing company that I wouldn't need to worry about many of the factors I listed above until I was earning a substantial amount of money from my business. I never got to that point. But when I stopped selling skin care products and retrained as a speaker, trainer, and coach, I had the opportunity to do a Certificate IV in Small Business Startup. Here I learnt all I would need to know to set up business as a sole trader and comply with all the relevant laws.

BUILDING A NETWORK MARKETING BUSINESS

Whether network marketing is how you will put your life's purpose into action or you are using it as an additional source of income, it is certainly a good way to earn income. However, I'd like to add some caveats to this statement.

1. **Pick a product or range of products you can use yourself, you are passionate about, and you can sell to the people in your network.**

    I loved the range of skin care products my network marketing company sold, and I still use them today. However, I wear very little makeup, partly because I find it hard to apply since I am blind, and partly because I'm just plain lazy. So, I never sold much makeup because I couldn't demonstrate it by applying it to my own skin, or that of my potential clients. When I was selling Tupperware many years ago, most of the people in my network were in their forties, fifties, and sixties, so they already had a collection of older Tupperware and weren't interested in buying any of the newer stuff I was trying to sell.

2. Make sure you have a big enough network to sell to.

The two aims of the network marketing model are: 1) to sell product, and 2) to recruit new people who can sell product. When you sell product, you earn commission on each sale. When you recruit someone to sell product, you earn a smaller commission on what they sell, as well as the commission you earn on your own sales.

The people who do best in network marketing are those who have access to, or can build, a large network of people who will continue to buy products, or who are willing to sell products themselves. I didn't succeed on either front. Most people in my network were in their forties and above, and they had established skin care routines they were not willing to change. Most of them also earned good incomes, so they were not interested in selling products to earn extra income. I do have a small number of clients who purchase products regularly, but certainly not enough to make an income I could live on.

3. Follow the system to the letter.

All network marketing companies have a system. This system has been developed and tested by the company founders, and it works. My problem was the system didn't work for me, so I tried to adapt it to my needs, which didn't work.

We were taught that the best way to find potential clients and recruits was to strike up conversations with a compliment such as "I love your shoes" or something similar. As a blind person, it is almost impossible for me to compliment someone on anything other than how they smell. We were also taught to approach mothers with babies or young children to talk to them about a flexible lifestyle where they could earn income whilst raising their children. Again, as a blind person, it was hard to identify these people unless, of course, their babies were crying, which meant it probably wasn't a good time for a chat!

Another way we were taught to promote our business was by putting posts on social media about our lifestyle, with appropriate pictures. It's not as easy for me as it is for a sighted person to pull out my phone and snap a selfie or take a quick video. This takes much more planning for me, so it is something I don't often do spontaneously.

EARNING INCOME FROM YOUR HOBBIES OR SKILLS

Whether network marketing is your side hustle or the way you put your life's purpose into action, it is possible to turn your hobbies and skills into income-earning opportunities. It could be as simple as earning some extra cash by cleaning or gardening for a friend or selling things you make through an Etsy store, or it could be as complicated as setting up a business.

My friend Raylee had a number of small children at home, so she decided to find something she could do from home that would earn her some income. She and her mother had made a number of quilts as a hobby, so they decided to buy a quilting machine to finish them off. If that were successful, they would turn their hobby into a business.

Raylee has now successfully been finishing quilts for clients for eleven years. Recently, she expanded her business to sell her own quilting patterns online.

Before deciding to turn your hobby or skill into a business, ask yourself the following questions:

1. **Will I still enjoy my hobby or skill if I have to do it every day and meet deadlines?**

   I absolutely love knitting and will do it every chance I get. But I certainly wouldn't want to knit for eight hours a day, five days a week, and I certainly wouldn't like to have to knit under pressure to meet deadlines.

2. **Do I need a licence or permit?**

   Many years ago, a group of wonderful ladies used to raise money for the Canberra Blind Society. They would often cater for functions and hold stalls where they would sell food to the public. They all had to have their kitchens inspected by our local health authority to make sure they met the standards required for kitchens that made food to be sold to the public.

3.   Will I require insurance?

Raylee has insurance for her quilting business that covers her if her quilting machine catches fire. Her insurance also covers anyone who comes into her house to drop off or pick up quilts.

4.   Do I have the time?

If your business is a side hustle, you will have to make sure you have enough time after work or on the weekends to do what you need to earn the income you want, while still allowing yourself time to spend with your friends and family, and get appropriate rest.

5.   Will there be startup costs to expand my skill or hobby into a business?

Raylee and her mother purchased a quilting machine, but they found it wasn't big enough for what they wanted to do, so they had to outlay a considerable amount of money to buy a bigger one.

6.   Is there a market for my product or service?

No matter how skilled you are, you won't be able to earn a cent if no one wants to buy what you have to offer. You may need to do some market research to determine a market exists for your product or service, and whether that market is big enough to earn you the income you need.

EXERCISE

1. In the space below, list all the skills or hobbies you could earn income from.

    _____

    _____

    _____

    _____

2. Considering the questions above, rank the skills or hobbies in question 1 according to how likely you would be to turn them into income-earning opportunities.

    _____

    _____

    _____

    _____

CREATING PASSIVE INCOME

Passive income is income that requires little to no effort to earn or maintain. The simplest example of passive income is interest earned on money put into a savings account with a bank. Passive income can also be earned through investing in property, shares in a managed fund, and even online sales.

I never understood the concept of passive income until I read Robert Kiyosaki's book *Rich Dad Poor Dad* and played his board game *CASHFLOW*. They revolutionised my ideas around income, and I would go so far as to say I think every child and every adult should read the book or play the game.

In the book and game, Kiyosaki teaches we should invest in assets and avoid putting money into liabilities. However, his definition of assets and liabilities is different from the traditional accounting definition. Kiyosaki defines an asset as something that will earn passive income, and a liability as something that doesn't. Examples of assets would be a bank account that earns interest, a share portfolio that pays dividends, a house that is bought and then sold for a profit, or an online course or product that people can purchase while you sleep. Kiyosaki would categorise a family home as a liability because it is not producing income.

These are only a few of the ways you can earn income. If you have the imagination, the will, and the skill, the sky is the limit.

SUMMARY

Managing your finances is important because you may need to cover the costs associated with discovering your life's purpose and putting it into action. You may also need a savings buffer to cover you if you are thinking of changing jobs.

Before you make any decisions that will affect your finances, it is important to take a snapshot of your financial position. To do this, work out how much you have and how much you need. Then, work out the consequences of any changes to your lifestyle you want to make. But before you do anything, seek financial and even legal advice.

A number of different options exist to earn additional sources of income. These include network marketing, turning your hobby or skill into an income-earning opportunity, and ways to earn passive income. But these are just a few examples.

A FINAL NOTE:

STEPPING INTO
YOUR NEW LIFE

Now that you have finished reading this book, what actions will you take? What goals will you set? What changes will you make to start putting your life's purpose into action?

I challenge you to take action. It's one thing to have discovered your life's purpose in your head; it's quite another to put it into action in your everyday life.

On the ten lines below, list the ten actions you will commit to taking in the next ninety days as a result of reading this book.

1. _____

2. _____

3. _____

4. _____

5. _____

6. _____

7. _____

8. _____

9. _____

10. _____

In this book, you've discovered what your life's purpose really is. You've learnt the three steps you need to take to discover your life's purpose. You've found out how to find the courage needed to take the next steps to put your life's purpose into action, and you've learnt how to deal with changes that will occur in your life as a result.

Finally, you've discovered how to lead yourself into your new purposeful future, how to master your mindset, and how to manage your finances.

I guarantee that if you do the work, follow the steps, and use the tools set out in this book, you, too, will discover your life's purpose and learn how to put it into action. You'll realise your life has meaning and significance, and you will feel like what you do every day matters. You'll know why you're here, and your life will be filled with excitement and possibility.

Now that you have read *Seeing by Vision, Not by Sight*, I encourage you to contact me. I'd love to hear what you liked and disliked about my book so I can improve it for the next printing. More importantly, I'd love to hear about you, your challenges, your obstacles, and your adversities so I can help you. In fact, I would like to offer you a complimentary, no-obligation, 30-60-minute consultation to see how I can help you.

My email address is Amanda@AmandaHeal.com.au and my mobile phone number is +61418515715. Please email me, or better still, text me with your name and time zone, and we will schedule your complimentary consultation.

I wish you all the very best on the journey to discovering your life's purpose and putting it into action. As Oscar-winning stage and costume designer Cecil Beaton said:

"Be daring, be different, be impractical, be anything that will assert integrity of purpose and imaginative vision against the play-it-safers, the creatures of the commonplace, the slaves of the ordinary."

Your friend,

ABOUT THE AUTHOR

Amanda Heal is a published author, professional keynote speaker, sought-after empowerment coach, podcaster, and entrepreneur. For years, she has inspired and encouraged clients and audiences alike to reach their full potential by finding hope, courage, and purpose.

Amanda is the sort of person who, if you tell her she can't do something, will usually find a way. You may not think that is a big deal, but she has been totally blind since birth, so what you might find easy often creates challenges for her that she overcomes.

Surviving premature birth in 1970 was the first of those challenges. At birth, she weighed just 0.750kg (1 lb 9 oz) and was 24.5cm (10") long.

Amanda was the first totally blind student to graduate with honours in Law from the Australian National University. She has climbed to an altitude of 3,210m/10,531 ft, in Nepal, retrained as a speaker and coach after being unexpectedly laid off at the end of a seventeen-year legal career, and is a podcaster and published author of multiple books.

Amanda has made a number of television appearances, including appearing on *ABC News* (Australia), *60 Minutes*, and *The Midday Show* (Australia). She has also done quite a number of radio interviews.

As a speaker, Amanda uses her life experiences to inspire and encourage audiences to take courageous action to overcome the challenges that keep them stuck so they can reach their full potential in work and life.

As a coach, Amanda helps people discover their life's purpose, overcome their limiting beliefs, and follow their dreams so they can celebrate rather than tolerate what they do each day.

Amanda currently lives in Canberra, Australia, with her guide dog Sadie and her budgie Maestro.

ABOUT AMANDA HEAL'S EMPOWERMENT COACHING

Do you ever feel that:

- Your life lacks meaning or significance?

- You work only to pay the bills, and your weekend is filled with chores?

- You don't know why you're here?

- There's more to life than this?

- Your life lacks direction or purpose?

- You're stuck in a rut or it's time for a change?

If you're struggling with any of the above and resonate with the material in this book, Amanda can help you with:

- Getting clarity on who you are, why you're here, and what you want to do with your life.
- Facing your fears, and finding the courage you need to do what you want to do.
- Taking courageous steps to reach your full potential in work and life.

Amanda would be thrilled to offer you a no-obligation, complimentary 30-60-minute empowerment coaching consultation by phone, via online chat, or in person if geographically possible. The best way to schedule it is to email her at Amanda@AmandaHeal.com.au or text her on +61418515715 with your name and your time zone so you can schedule your call.

ABOUT AMANDA HEAL'S PODCAST

Whether you are a lawyer, health care professional, teacher, or work in any other profession, this podcast is for you. Amanda Heal, your host, will share her own experiences as a totally blind lawyer facing and overcoming the normal everyday challenges of professional life, and she will reveal how she eventually left the law and reinvented herself in a completely different career, which she loves. She'll share stories of overcoming disillusionment with work, bullying, being laid off, and career change, and she will also interview experts on these and related topics to encourage and inspire you to take courageous steps to reach your *full* potential.

To listen, just search for "TheDoWhatYouLovePodcast" on your favourite podcast platform, or visit the podcast page at https://TheDoWhatYouLovePodcast.com. If you like what you hear, please don't forget to subscribe, and also leave a review.

BOOK AMANDA HEAL TO SPEAK AT YOUR NEXT EVENT

Whether your audience is 10 or 10,000, in Australia or abroad, Amanda Heal can deliver a customised message of inspiration and encouragement for your next meeting or conference. Amanda understands that your audience doesn't want to be taught; they want to hear stories of inspiration, achievement, and real people stepping into their destinies.

Amanda Heal's speaking philosophy is to entertain, inspire, and encourage your audience with passion and stories proven to help people achieve extraordinary results. If you are looking for a memorable speaker who will leave your audience wanting more, book Amanda Heal today.

To see a highlight video of Amanda Heal and find out whether she is available to speak at your next event, visit her site at the address below, and then contact her by phone or email to schedule a complimentary pre-speech interview.

https://PurposeVisionFuture.com

Amanda@AmandaHeal.com.au

Mobile +61418515715

www.ingramcontent.com/pod-product-compliance
Lightning Source LLC
Chambersburg PA
CBHW071850090426
42811CB00004B/553